SACRED
WORK

Planting Cultures of Radical
Loving Care in America

ERIE CHAPMAN

Author of *Radical Loving Care*

Caregiver's Edition Field Guide
Including:
Five Steps to Culture Change
Fifteen Work Tools
A List of America's Most Caring Hospitals
Examples of Loving Charities that Practice Sacred Work

SACRED WORK

Planting Cultures of Radical Loving Care in America

Live from love, not fear.

For one human being to love another is perhaps the most difficult task of all, the epitome, the ultimate test. It is that striving for which all other striving is merely preparation.

—Rainer Maria Rilke

Printed in the United States of America

Library of Congress Control Number: 2006925373

ISBN 0-9747366-7-8

Fourth Printing - February 2008

Published by:
The Baptist Healing Trust (BHT)
1919 Charlotte Avenue, Suite 320
Nashville, Tennessee 37203
615-284-8271
www.healinghospital.org

Book Design & Layout:
Bill Kersey
KerseyGraphics
Nashville, TN

Printed by:
Vaughan Printing Company
Nashville, TN

Cover Painting: Highmore, Joseph The Good Samaritan, 1744. Tate Gallery, London, Great Britain. Photo credit: Tate Gallery, London.

ACKNOWLEDGMENTS

I offer special thanks to all of the members of the Healing Trust team:

Virgil Moore—Chair of the Board, Baptist Healing Trust. The best Board Chair I've ever worked with and a Southern gentleman in the very best sense.

Keith Hagan, M.D.—Chair of the Program and Grants Committee. Thank you for being a model of ideal balance between clinical excellence and endless compassion.

All the members of the Board of the Healing Trust for their belief that foundations need to do more than just hand out checks to grantees: that they need to be true ministries of caring.

And to (in alphabetical order):

Matt Deeb, who transcends his role as accounting manager to provide insight, advice, and presence to all aspects of the Trust's work. Who says accountants don't have a sense of humor?

Kristen Keely-Dinger, whose hard work, sense of justice, and deep commitment enable the fair evaluation of grant applications, and whose intelligent aid helps charities become their best.

Junie Ewing, M.Div., Ph.D., who combines academic intelligence and analytical skills with the ability to organize the rest of us.

Rollie Mains, a renaissance thinker whose genius transcends music, enabling him to journey into the stratosphere of complex philosophy to find its gold and deliver it into our hands.

Dawn Meadows-Thrasher, whose world-class help has enabled the delivery of books and materials to every state in the union, and whose charm is unmatched.

Kristin O'Keefe, whose intelligence and kind heart shine through her quiet presence.

Catherine Self, a world-class teacher whose energy, charm, and insight help create sacred encounters every day.

Gary Vacca, whose kind grace, warm laugh, and genuine spirituality are a gift to all who meet him.

Stephanie Zembar, whose steady hand, trustworthiness, and deep competence are so important to the successful operation of the Trust.

And to **Jan Keeling** for her remarkably constructive help and kindness in the editing of this work, and **Bill Kersey,** the best book designer I've ever met.

Dedication

This book is dedicated to America's caregivers, the millions of anonymous people who, in the midst of long days and lonely nights, bring the love of the Samaritan to those in need. And to Marian, Tracy, Jeff, Nick, Frank, Steve, Cathy, and Mark. Thank you for your friendship, your loyalty, and your gift of loving leadership in this world.

CONTENTS

PART ONE
The Season of Choosing
Laying the Foundation

PART TWO
The Season of Learning
Essential Tools

PART THREE
The Season of Doing
Concept to Practice

PART FOUR
The Season of Being
Presence and the Sacred Encounter

THOUGHTS ON LOVE
AND SACRED WORK

That Love is all there is, Is all we know of love.

—Emily Dickinson

Love, love, love, that is the soul of genius.

—Attributed to Wolfgang Amadeus Mozart

I think of compassion as the fundamental religious experience and, unless that is there, you have nothing.

—Joseph Campbell, *The Power of Myth*

Love costs all we are
And will ever be
But it is only love
That can set us free

— Maya Angelou

One thing I asked of the Lord,
that will I seek after:
to live in the house of the Lord
all the days of my life,
to behold the beauty of the Lord,
and to inquire in his temple.

—From Psalm 27

THE GOLDEN THREAD OF THE HEALING TRADITION: HISTORIC ROOTS OF LOVING CARE

JEWISH

What is hateful to you, do not do to your neighbor. This is the whole Torah; all the rest is commentary. Go and learn it. (Hillel, Talmud, Shabbath 31a)

You shall not take vengeance or bear a grudge against any of your people, but you shall love your neighbor as yourself: I am the LORD. (Leviticus 19:18)

HINDU

Love thy neighbor, for he is yourself. (The Vedas)

THE BUDDHA

Teach this triple truth to all: A generous heart, kind speech and a life of service and compassion are the things which renew humanity.

ISLAM

Do good—to parents, kinsfolk, orphans, those in need, neighbors who are near, neighbors who are strangers, the companion by your side, the wayfarer. (Holy Koran An-Nisa 4.36)

CHRISTIAN

Love one another. (John 13:34)

THE PARABLE OF THE GOOD SAMARITAN

Luke 10:25-37

25 Just then a lawyer stood up to test Jesus. "Teacher," he said, "what must I do to inherit eternal life?" 26 He said to him, "What is written in the law? What do you read there?" 27 He answered, "You shall love the Lord your God with all your heart, and with all your soul, and with all your strength, and with all your mind; and your neighbor as yourself." *[italics added]* 28 And he said to him, "You have given the right answer; do this, and you will live." 29 But wanting to justify himself, he asked Jesus, "And who is my neighbor?"

30 Jesus replied, "A man was going down from Jerusalem to Jericho, and fell into the hands of robbers, who stripped him, beat him, and went away, leaving him half dead. 31 Now by chance a priest was going down that road; and when he saw him, he passed by on the other side. 32 So likewise a Levite, when he came to the place and saw him, passed by on the other side. 33 But a Samaritan while traveling came near him; and when he saw him, he was moved with pity. 34 He went to him and bandaged his wounds, having poured oil and wine on them. Then he put him on his own animal, brought him to an inn, and took care of him. 35 The next day he took out two denarii, gave them to the innkeeper, and said, 'Take care of him; and when I come back, I will repay you whatever more you spend.'

36 Which of these three, do you think, was a neighbor to the man who fell into the hands of the robbers?" 37 He said, "The one who showed him mercy." Jesus said to him, "Go and do likewise."

THE CORE OF OUR HUMANITY

Spirituality means waking up. Most people, even though they don't know it, are asleep.

— Father Anthony de Mello (1931–1987)

A recent story on *CBS News Sunday Morning* reported on the deterioration of respect for the elderly in Japan. The situation is so desperate, the reporter said, that mechanical pets, or robotic caregivers, have been developed to mimic warmth and human kindness in the care of old people. The robots make soothing sounds. They are stroked and petted by institutionalized senior citizens so anxious for love that they accept its imitation by a machine.

Does this story represent the devolution of humanity toward a world so emptied of human Loving Care, or so tired of giving it, that we create robots programmed to *mimic* acts of kindness? Will our reward for living a long time become our delivery into the hands of machines, our last days spent tethered to sophisticated technology instead of in the loving arms of our family or friends? This Orwellian nightmare has been in place for many years for those unlucky patients who, unable or unwilling to choose hospice care, end up dying in hospital critical-care units. For these patients, the last sound they hear in this world may be the honking alarm of a monitor that reports the last beat of their hearts.

Part of the value in the story from Japan is its implicit affirmation that kindness is so essential that scientists are trying to find ways to mimic it.

Simultaneously, of course, this development demeans kindness's unique quality by suggesting that it *can* be effectively mimicked. And therein lies the real impact of this story. It is the most recent warning that we may be on the verge of yielding to robots one of the few remaining things that distinguish us as human beings—our ability to give Loving Care to those in need.

THE COURAGE TO LOVE

Cultures of Sacred Work are marked not only by the absence of fear, but by the presence of love.

In the later pages of this book I will talk about the courage required to be present to someone in need. Here, at the beginning, I want to emphasize that *every* aspect of Sacred Work, including its initiation into your life, requires courage.

One of the greatest thinkers in modern history, Paul Tillich, writes in his book *The Courage to Be,* "Not conformity but differentiation is the end of the ways of God. Self-affirmation of one's uniqueness and acceptance of the demands of one's individual nature are the right courage to be."

It requires courage for us to assert our individuality against the forces of conformity and the status quo that live in hospitals and the rest of the charitable world. Tillich also writes, "Power is the possibility a being has to actualize itself against the resistance of other beings." This does not mean that we are compelled to alienate ourselves from our colleagues. Instead, it suggests that love calls us to do more than the status quo asks—that we can be models of compassion and competence whether or not we receive encouragement from the world around us.

Every time we choose to treat an interaction as a sacred encounter we are expressing our courage to love, because sacred encounters call upon us to be vulnerable. We need to open the ears of our hearts in order to hear the real needs of the person before us. The forces of comfort and conformity may shout to us, "Don't bother. Don't make the effort." But if we listen to the voice of love, it will always summon us to offer our gifts of love as a salve to ease the pain of another.

THE HISTORY OF SACRED WORK

Every religious and humanitarian tradition is grounded in a single idea: Love is about serving the other above the self. We have souls. Yet much of our capacity to love may be lying dormant – either buried below the scar tissue of life, or simply undiscovered. Accordingly, loving those who seem "unlovable" may seem counterintuitive. But it is the highest expression of our humanity.

The parable of the Good Samaritan comes from the Christian tradition. It is a story told by Jesus to illustrate not only kindness toward strangers but the whole notion of love as a pattern of thought and action that goes beyond simple compassion. The Samaritan tends to the wounds of the injured man with the best skills available to him. He then lifts his patient onto the back of his animal and takes him to an inn where he pays for this stranger's care with his own money. These acts would be more than enough to satisfy most people's standards of deep caring. Yet the Samaritan goes further by leaving money with the innkeeper to care for the man and promising to return to cover any extra costs that may be incurred. All of this is for a complete stranger.

This parable of the Samaritan's encounter with a stranger offers a foundation for thinking of work as sacred. Love is God's work, for God is Love.

- Sacred work is based on the idea that *every action needs to be grounded in loving intention.* Caregiving is about ministering to the deepest needs of others. It is far more than customer service (a phrase which should be eliminated from the lexicon of all charities as demeaning the nature of need and love). We need no other rule than the one that tells us to love our neighbors.

But human nature is deeply complex. Grounding our actions in love is as complicated as the rule is simple.

SACRED WORK AS UNIVERSAL AND INCLUSIVE

God is present by Love alone.

—Thomas Traherne (1636–1674)

It is not the primary goal of this work to teach or advance religion. But part of its objective is to spread understanding of the *universality* of the notion of charitable work as sacred. Loving care is a practice found in all enlightened ways of thinking about human relationships. Samaritan stories are part of the golden thread of love that weaves through the history of every great faith as well as the humanitarian tradition.

It is useful to understand the depth of the roots of Loving Care. Historians agree that the first evidence of civilization arose in Mesopotamia (current-day Iraq) among the Sumerians nearly six thousand years ago. Acts of kindness surely did not begin with the development of religion, so we may assume that the golden thread of love is more ancient than any current organized faith.

The cuneiform writing of the Sumerians tells us they believed in multiple gods. Like the multiple gods of the Greeks and Romans, these gods became complicated and confusing to those attempting to discern meaning in life. Multiple gods were also a source of *divisiveness* among those who backed one set of gods over another.

Although an ancient Egyptian monarch advanced the notion of one god (called Aten), the idea didn't endure. It took the Jews to unify all gods into the concept of one great God. Love of one God lived at the core of the then-new faith. Although early Jews believed that this God was exclusive to them, this thinking evolved into an understanding of one God for all humankind.

The development of human understanding of a single God is important because it has helped to *unify* all faiths and all of the humanitarian tradition. Faith traditions may have different views of many things, but there is unity around the banner of love as the highest expression of human beings towards each other. If there is one God for all and we are all children of that God, then we are all brothers and sisters. Our ability to love, and our need for love, unifies us all.

HAS CIVILIZATION ADVANCED LOVE?

How has the idea of love changed over the centuries? In early Jewish culture, love of God was described as love of neighbor. Later, as the Samaritan parable tells us, love of neighbor came to mean love of *any* other person. Jesus called his followers to do something radical, to love their enemies—a practice I rarely see followed by those who claim Christianity as their faith. Gandhi, a Hindu, once made a telling comment about this matter in the 1940s: "Christianity is a beautiful faith, but I have not seen many Christians practicing it."

History demonstrates that tyrants have often used religion as a divisive rather than a unifying force. For centuries, Moslems, Jews, and Christians lived in relative harmony in Spain. They were unified by the belief that they were all "people of the book." Unfortunately, King Ferdinand and Queen

Isabella took power in the late 15th century and rapidly sought to force their notion of the Christian faith on all Spaniards. On the very day Columbus sailed off on his first voyage, Jews and Moslems who had refused to convert were forced onto ships and exiled from their country.

Recent history, including the behavior of religious zealots in the Middle East, suggests that much of the world has yet to learn the core teaching of every major faith. We are to love our neighbors, not persecute them.

Whether love is better expressed now than it was in ancient times is a troubling issue. There is no question that we have made great scientific progress. It is measurable in numbers of lives saved from the grasp of once-deadly diseases. It is expressed in statistics reporting our lengthening average lifespan. But has humankind's rising scientific sophistication improved the expression of Loving Care?

The worst war the world has ever seen ended only sixty years ago. More recently, genocide has scarred the world in Serbia and Bosnia, in Rwanda, and in Darfur.

A recent three-year study by the Canadian-based Human Security Centre reports that over the past dozen years the world has experienced a declining number of wars and a lower number of deaths due to military actions. Encouraging as this may seem, it is not at all clear that this means we behave toward each other in more civilized and human ways. Other data in the report indicates a sharp increase in terrorist activity and guerilla warfare, implying that the forces of violence may have simply changed tactics, switching from old-style conventional warfare to underground movements.

MISSION FRAUD:
THE DANGER OF A MISSION/MARGIN DICHOTOMY

In the midst of global challenges, what is the current state of organizations whose missions invoke the language of Loving Care—contemporary hospitals and charities? We may have learned not to chain the insane to prison walls, but have we yet learned to treat them humanely and respectfully? We have created corridors of efficiency for the processing of hospital patients, but are we treating them with the dignity to which all people, especially the ill, are entitled? We deliver more financial aid to the poor, but are they treated with dignity? Do most of us engaged in charitable work yet appreciate that service to the vulnerable is a privilege, that those who come before us made meek by illness or abuse are blessing our caregiving as sacred?

These questions answer themselves. We are not doing nearly as well caring for each other as we could. A big reason for this is that the leadership of America's charities is failing in its responsibility to take care of caregivers. I'm not talking about pay and benefits, which will always be inadequate. I'm addressing the level of emotional and spiritual support that leaders give to first line staff, and the commitment of time and energy they devote to caring rather than fussing with bottom-line margins.

Several years ago, the leader of a large, faith-based healthcare system said, with respect to the role of the money needed to operate the organization: "No margin, no mission." Sadly, this phrase became a sort of battle cry for certain hospital leaders, financial officers, and board members. They used it to belittle the role of mission and shove it to the sidelines. In the midst of nascent efforts to advance Loving Care by some of America's best mission officers, a given leader would sniff, "Hey, no margin, no mission." Organizational energy was shifted back to business operations and mission was abandoned to token meetings of chaplains and other caregivers who dutifully, and sometimes passionately, begged the organization to remember its focus on care for the vulnerable.

The fraudulent nature of this approach became apparent when some of the organizations grumbling about margins turned out to have coffers filled with billions of dollars and eight- and nine-figure margins. It is reasonable for charitable organizations to generate margins adequate to support mission and to strengthen the organization. It is unethical for these organizations to continue to offer themselves as places of Loving Care when the predominant agenda items all focus on finance and technology.

A TIME FOR ANGER?

The truth is that the entire system of charitable care has slipped *out of balance*. In hospitals, technology and business have become monstrous gods crushing first line workers and converting them, in the eyes of many leaders, into automatons or units of expense.

Should you doubt the degree to which hospital leaders have taken their eye off the ball, consider the results of a recent survey of healthcare leaders conducted by the American College of Healthcare Executives (ACHE). Under the headline "What really matters most," *Modern Healthcare* reported in their January 9, 2006, issue that the number one worry, by a huge margin, in the minds of CEOs was "Financial Challenges." Fully two-thirds of the respondents listed "Financial Challenges" first (67%). "Quality" ranked fifth (23%) and "Patient Safety" sixth (20%). The mission of Loving Care for patients did not make the list at all. It was simply not on the radar screen for healthcare leaders even though widespread review shows that: 1) Loving Care is a part of most mission statements, and 2) hospitals routinely fail in its delivery and pay little attention to it in training and in meetings.

No wonder we fear the treatment we and our loved ones might receive should we have to don a patient gown.

In other charities, bureaucracy and the enormous challenge of caring for the socially and developmentally oppressed has left many support-givers feeling numb, their caring capability buried in paperwork and exhaustion.

We can find an example of this in a governmental organization that parallels a charity in its responsibility to care for the vulnerable. A recent news exposé reveals that the Veterans Administration (VA), by its own analysis, routinely delivers to its clients wrong or incomplete answers in a rude and uncaring way. If you're a veteran it means you served your country, sometimes risking your life to defend its sacred values. If you're a veteran who needs a helpful answer from your government, you've got only about a thirty percent chance of getting a reliable answer delivered in a respectful way.

Effective leadership and programs to help caregivers heal can reverse much of this problem. To see that a big government agency doesn't have to be like that, take a look at the Ohio Department of Health under the leadership of Nick Baird, M.D. When Nick took over his responsibilities he didn't say to himself, "Now I'm running a government agency, I'm dealing with a bunch of bureaucrats, and there's not much I can do to change things." Instead, he tackled the challenges before him using many of the principles he learned as Medical Director at Riverside Methodist and OhioHealth working with our team. For many years now he has engaged leadership teams and first line staff in dialogues on how to improve service throughout the state. He has made countless visits to outposts of the agency all over Ohio, listening to his staff and cheering them on. The result is a huge government agency that is, according to outsiders who regularly deal with it, one of the most service-oriented organizations they have encountered. Nick didn't do it alone. But his has been the catalyzing leadership that led to the creation of a culture of respect and Loving Care.

The VA fails because both its leadership and its systems are in disarray and no one will step forward with creative leadership. A VA employee on the phone with a veteran has been poorly trained by uninspired leaders, is working for low government pay, and has heard the same kinds of questions over and over. Since the employee feels anonymous, unappreciated, undertrained, and unsupported, why should he or she care about the voice on the other end of the line? It's not that none of the employees are trying to do the right thing, because many are trying. But this segment of the VA has developed a culture of mediocrity. It's hard to practice excellence in such an environment.

Many of America's hospitals and charities have fallen into the same rut. If they were honest, some hospitals would remove the mission statement from the wall—especially the part that talks about caring—and replace it with a set of lines that might go something like this:

- Welcome to Saint General's Hospital.
- Got a problem? We'll take our best shot at fixing it.
- You can stay in one of our rooms at a nightly rate higher than any hotel in the country.
- Note: There may be a stranger in the room with you, and we are not responsible for any noises he or she might make.
- We will decide what you wear to bed. Note: Don't even think about wearing your own pajamas. Do expect to lie on a stretcher for a long time in a long hallway half-naked. Enjoy the fluorescent ceiling lights.
- We expect to get paid as much as we can for what we do to you.
- If we make a mistake, we'll try again—and we'll charge you again, too.
- If you're unhappy, talk to our customer relations people in the basement. Although they may have no power, authority, or medical training, they will probably smile.
- Alternatively, you can sue us.
- Have a nice day and night.

This may sound like a bitter indictment from someone who has run hospitals for a quarter-century. It is. I am angry at myself for not doing more to correct the problems I saw and continue to see. And I am angry at the leaders of our hospital and charity system for not committing more effort to solving problems that are clearly correctable. I hope you are angry, too.

Anger may be an essential part of the process we need to go through to generate the sense of injustice needed to create real reform. But don't stop there. Beyond simple anger are constructive answers. It is time that we look into the face of this challenge and grow places worthy of our lofty missions. The millions of people who come for care every day and night are hoping and praying for something much better. Every one of them deserves better than what most of the system is giving. Charities that can't deliver on their own missions should lose their tax-exempt status and face the possibility of closing down. Those charities that are truly living their mission need to be celebrated and held up as models from which the rest can learn.

It's important to note that restoring charities to balance does not mean abandoning technology or business or good operating systems. It means returning love to its proper place at the *foundation* of all charitable work. It means weaving respect and caring into all business and technological interplays. It means delivering effective care with kindness and compassion for those in need.

A TIME FOR NEW GRACE: WHY CHARITY WORK IS SACRED

The old Samaritan stories are meant to teach us not only that love sits at the center of humanity, but that love can be present in all people and all things. As all faiths teach, God is Love. An ancient statement passed on from a Delphic oracle by Erasmus and hung by Carl Jung over the doorway of his office says: *Vocatus at que non vocatus dues ad erit.* It means: *Called or not called, God is present.* As God is always present, so, therefore, is Love.

This fundamental truth leads us to the heart of why charitable work is sacred. Human life is about relationships. Without the guidance of love, humanity is degraded to lower forms of living. Without love, human life itself lacks meaning.

The mental picture of work as sacred points us to the necessity of love in relationships marked by acute and chronic human need. The whole concept of charity flows from the call of weakened human beings who need help to stronger ones who have the ability to give it.

America's hospitals and charities, like those around the rest of the world, were founded to organize the most effective delivery of this need. From the beginning, the idea of a hospital was that care could be best delivered if the sick and wounded were gathered together under one roof to be cared for by those with special skills and strength and a commitment to caring. That was the role of the church in helping to found the first hospitals in western civilization: to provide places where *hospitality* would be given to those in need—most especially the poor—and that hospitality meant compassion. The very word hospital is drawn from the word hospitality.

Up until the last hundred years, compassion seemed in good supply, delivered through the kind hands of caregivers who were poor in technology but rich in love. As forces of technology and business advanced, the balance gradually moved the other way. In most of today's American hospitals, the forces that dominate are not love and compassion but bureaucracy, business, and a technology that is so dazzling we have, in some instances, yielded our humanity to it.

We would all rather have surgery done with the most modern techniques and equipment. But does this mean human beings must ignore the gifts of mercy that every vulnerable human seeks? Shouldn't technology itself be guided by a loving hand rather than the hand of one who cares nothing about the patient being treated?

LOVE'S RARITY IN CHARITY

● *How many leave hospitals healed of their physical illness but hurt in their feelings by the impersonal treatment they received?*
—Henri Nouwen, *Reaching Out:*
The Three Movements of the Spiritual Life

Human feelings are ripped and trampled on in the machinery of the medical-industrial complex. And these are not only the feelings of patients, but of their caregivers as well. Nouwen suggests that the depersonalization caused by "technocratic streamlining" has led to "interpersonal violence." Rude and callous treatment by leaders of caregivers and by caregivers of each other and patients has led some caregivers to, as poet David Whyte says, "leave their hearts in the parking lot" before they come into work.

The organized delivery of Loving Care in America's charities, especially in its hospitals, is in dire need of reform. The evidence of its absence becomes undeniable when we look at the single most important aspect of service: the *encounter* between patient and caregiver. Caregiver, here, means *any* member of the support-giving team, from housekeeper to CEO, from nurse to administrator, from social worker to food service worker, even from vendor to salesperson.

The need for change should be obvious to everyone. Walk into the emergency department of any major hospital in the country (and most of the smaller ones) with a pain in your side. You are now headed for your first encounter. What are your chances of being greeted with the kindness and mercy needed by a human being in pain? Every American has come to expect the first words out of the admitting clerk's mouth: "Name, address, insurance card?"

Whatever the exact words (since new laws now restrict the kinds of information gathered in the initial encounter), the point is what the clerk is *not* saying, what she or he is not expressing in the eyes. She or he is unlikely to express any concern for your agony, to say something like, "I'm sorry to see you're in pain. Maybe I can get this information quickly," or "Let me run get a nurse for you."

This kind of breakdown in the core encounters the vulnerable have each day and night with caregivers will not be solved by something as superficial as customer service. Patients dying of cancer or women in the midst of a hard childbirth don't want *customer* service, they want *loving* service. They want the kind of caring we want for our mothers and sisters and brothers and certainly for our children. Shouldn't everyone who has fallen into the mire of vulnerability be entitled to love?

Over the course of a five-day stay in a typical hospital, a patient will have hundreds of encounters with caregivers. Many will be polite, some will even be considerate. But when loving encounters occur, it is often in spite of the demands of the medical-industrial complex, not because of it. The mission statements that adorn every hospital and charity in the country are, in most cases, nothing more than fraudulent representations of a level of caring that emerges, if at all, in random fashion.

Hospitals and charities have a responsibility to recognize that the people in their care, including the caregivers themselves, need to be treated with a respect grounded in love. It will take a revelation, followed by a revolution, to restore the kind of balance that will leave you and me feeling our loved ones will be loved as well as "fixed" when they enter the health-care system.

INCLUDING PRICKLY PEOPLE, EXCLUDING BULLIES

The arms of Loving Care extend love to all. And it is important to know that the concept of Sacred Work is not some kind of *Mary Poppins* culture where everyone is expected to be happy and cheerful at all times. The delivery of Loving Care assumes firmness, discipline, and high-level competence. Cultures of Sacred Work may include personalities that some would describe as "prickly." Loving skeptics are essential for real balance.

At the same time, a loving culture cannot tolerate the presence of bullying, fear-based behavior by caregivers at any level. It is the responsibility of leadership to ensure that bullies are either reformed or removed from the environment. Chronic unreasonable negativity has no place as well, since it darkens the quality of energy needed to advance love.

The Firelight Window®, described both in *Radical Loving Care* and in this book on pages 36–38, is the recommended model for leaders who want to determine a process to address this issue. It may be the best device to help leaders in guiding errant partners toward reform or respectful removal from the organization

WHAT'S IN IT FOR ME?

In a book about Loving Care, this question may seem out of place. My colleague Rollie Mains insists that human nature is such that this question needs to be addressed. He's right. After all, it's not uncommon to hear: "I'm not getting paid enough to make all this effort to change the status quo."

This attitude leads to a central question: Why are you doing what you're doing? Here are some possible answers. The ranking of these choices is always interesting, especially when applied to employees in love-based cultures.

1. **Paycheck.** Lots of people make the mistake of listing this as number one. Everyone needs some level of pay to maintain a reasonable quality of life. But study after study (including a fascinating analysis of the chronic unhappiness of many lottery winners) demonstrates that once our basic needs have been met, extra pay doesn't make much of a difference in our happiness level. Will a culture of Loving Care generate better pay? Not necessarily. But there is a good chance your organization will be more successful and, therefore, that your job will be more secure.

2. **Benefits.** This sounds like #1 but it's a little different. Some people come to work at large charities not for the pay but for the benefits.

3. **Passion to Serve Others.** Whether or not this is #1 on your list, your patients are hoping it is #1. No one served by a charity wants to be served by someone who is lackadaisical about the work. The best and happiest partners in healthcare routinely put this first. Still, they are not, unless they are financially independent, willing to work for free.

4. **The Positive Reputation and Quality of My Organization.** This is a more powerful motivator than many people realize. Some people like to work for places like Harvard, The Mayo Clinic, The White House, Disney, Southwest Airlines, The New York Yankees (or Boston Red Sox), CNN, or the United Nations simply because of the enormous reputation these organizations have. The names suggest both a fine history and high quality. Most of us want to be associated with high quality. We want to be part of a "winning team"—an organization we feel good about. This is equally true of smaller, local organizations. In any given city, each charity has a reputation. People are drawn to work for organizations with good reputations. Organizations with bad reputations repel the best talent. (At Riverside Methodist Hospital in the early '90s, we developed such a positive reputation as an employee-friendly organization that one year, nearly 30,000 people applied for 800 job openings. Our employee turnover, in a six-thousand-person organization, dropped into the single digits. And our good reputation kept feeding upon itself in positive ways, until different leadership came in and squandered much of this goodwill.)

5. **My Supervisor.** Survey after survey shows that the biggest determinant of employee satisfaction is "treatment by supervisor."

6. **My Fellow Workers.** For relationship-oriented people, this element is tremendously important.

7. **Proximity to Home.** Some people actually list this in first place.

8. **The Mission of the Organization.** Matched with #3, this can be a key magnet element in loving-care cultures. Consider the enormous ability of the Southern Christian Leadership Conference (SCLC) to attract thousands of capable people during the leadership of Dr.

Martin Luther King, Jr. Many people took lower-paying jobs just to be a part of this effort. The same was true of NASA in the '60s and into the '70s. NASA's Moon Mission was powerful enough to attract numerous talented people.

9. **Belief That This Work Will Improve the Quality of My Life in My Work Setting.** Anyone who has ever worked in a loving-care culture knows that this can easily become #1 for them. Combine it with #s 3 and 8, and you have the ideal top three reasons loving cultures attract talent. The reason pay slips down the list is that Loving Caregivers realize that the difference between one paycheck and another in most charities isn't very large. Would you leave a Loving Care environment to work in a fear-based culture for an extra fifty cents an hour? Some people do this and they always regret it.

10. **A Love-Based Culture Will Generate Better Outcomes for Everyone Involved with the Organization Than Will a Fear-Based Culture.** I will describe some of these outcomes, on pages 23–26.

11. **It's the Right Thing to Do.** Funny that I listed this last, huh? I put it last because, although everybody says they want to engage in Loving Care because it's the right thing to do, many surveys suggest that most caregivers find this an inadequate answer to the question: What's in it for me? In love-based cultures, the fact that such work is the right thing to do can become the only answer many people need.

REGAINING BALANCE

Our goal is not to demean the role of paychecks as motivators. Nor is it to degrade the importance of technology or business. And our objective in criticizing the quality of much charity work today is certainly not to criticize America's overworked and underpaid caregivers.

The goal is to issue a clarion call for balance. *The caregiver-patient encounter has broken down because the leader-caregiver relationship is broken.* The break is so bad that you and I are loathe to trust our mothers or any other loved ones to the system without our active intervention.

Even shepherding of a patient by a loving expert is no guarantee of success. National health leader Don Berwick, M.D., found this out when he tried to help his wife through a process of treatment at one of America's best-known hospitals. He found that even with his expert intervention, doctors, nurses, and other caregivers made an astonishing array of errors, and often seemed insensible to his wife's suffering.

The reasons for this are manifold. But caregivers make mistakes in part because they feel rushed, dehumanized, and undersupported in their challenging work, thus losing their motivation to perform successfully.

The source of the problem lies not in technology or in business but in human encounters. Better-motivated leaders and staff, people who truly view their work as sacred, will generate better and more effective systems of care.

If we are to answer your question about what's in this for *you*, remember that the aim is to create a better workplace—a place you would love to come to each day because the mission of excellence is being lived out, because you can live your passion, and because you are affirmed for the work you are doing by leaders whose first interest is supporting you in your efforts to do Sacred Work.

• **Here is the goal:** to create continuous love-based encounters between the vulnerable and all the people serving them—directly or indirectly.

• **Here is the pathway:** the development of love-based (*vs.* fear-based) cultures in which charity work is understood as sacred.

• **Here is the catalyst:** enlightened and effective leadership.

• **Here is the guaranteed outcome:** superior systems of care in which patients are loved, respected, and cared for with the best possible treatment.

FINDING YOUR YES

My whole life has hung too long upon a partial victory.
—William Carlos Williams

It has taken a lifetime of work and study for me to discover and become clear about my own, personal Yes in life. At age sixty-two, I am more certain than ever that the Yes in my work life (against all the No's and negativity in the world) is the Yes of advancing the mission of Loving Care to and on behalf of America's charitable caregivers.

It all seems so obvious to me now. What choice could be better than a dedication to advancing Loving Care? But for so many years, my life echoed the language of the Williams poem—it hung upon a partial victory. Holding back on the release of my full potential, I found myself dreaming of alternative pathways in life, other careers, other ways to use my life energy.

This quotation from C.S. Lewis, brought to my attention by Rollie Mains, is as powerful as anything I've seen in describing the choice of Love:

> To love at all is to be vulnerable. Love anything, and your heart will certainly be wrung and possibly be broken. If you want to make sure of keeping it intact, you must give your heart to no one, not even to an animal. Wrap it carefully round with hobbies and little luxuries; avoid all entanglements; lock it up safe in the casket or coffin of your selfishness. But in that casket—safe, dark, motionless, airless—it will change. It will not be broken; it will become unbreakable, impenetrable, irredeemable. The alternative to tragedy, or at least to the risk of tragedy, is damnation. The only place outside Heaven where you can be perfectly safe from all the dangers and perturbations of love is Hell.

—C.S. Lewis, *The Four Loves*

To love is be vulnerable, which is why it takes courage. But there is no more important Yes in our lives than the Yes we bring to Love.

What is the Yes in your life? As you survey the many parts of the world where you see No's—the violence portrayed on television news, the violence you see in the way so many people around you may treat each other, the bleak No of people who have given up on their lives and their work—where do you see your clearest Yes?

As a caregiver, the people you support are hoping you will say Yes to them, Yes to meeting their needs with the special genius of your own loving gifts. One of the greatest discoveries available to all of us is the revelation of the astonishing capacity we have to express love to others (and ourselves), and how much of it we have left unused.

The gift of this book is to offer you a set of practices that will help you mine your own gifts. What's in it for you is the certain discovery that if you choose to do this hard work, you will be rewarded with riches far greater than anything that can come to you through a paycheck or benefits package. You will have found the greatest treasure of all—the meaning and purpose of your life.

PART ONE

The Season of Choosing

Laying the Foundation

I am convinced that the best management process for today's environment is participative management based on covenantal relationships.
—Max Depree

CHARITY WORK AS A SACRAMENT AND A COVENANT

Whenever the tissue of life is woven of legalistic relationships, this creates an atmosphere of spiritual mediocrity that paralyzes men's best impulses.

—Alexander Solzhenitsyn,
Address to the Class of 1978 Harvard University

How we describe our work determines how we think and act in the place where we spend two-thirds of our waking lives. It is also reflects how we feel and how we see those around us.

The words sacrament and covenant are typically applied to religious ritual, and it can be risky to use such words in settings that pride themselves on being science-based and "objective." The goal of this work is not to evangelize a denomination, but to construct a helpful bridge over which useful ideas from the world of faith can cross, and inform the practice of healthcare.

Sacraments are sacred because they are practices that bring us closer to God's love. Covenants are pacts we make that include God (and, therefore, love). The late, great American businessman and renowned author Max DePree (former CEO of the Herman Miller Company) wrote that "Covenantal relationships reflect unity and grace and poise. They are an expression of the sacred nature of relationships . . . Words such as love, warmth, personal chemistry are certainly pertinent."

What if we integrated sacramental and covenantal thinking into the way we approach our work? As Mother Teresa, Gandhi, and Martin Luther

King have demonstrated, loving work on behalf of the poor automatically takes on a sacramental quality because the engagement of love naturally engages the presence of God.

Everyone who does charitable work—whether they see themselves as a leader, food service worker, secretary, housekeeper, social worker, nurse, or accountant—is a caregiver. You, as a caregiver, have chosen the most meaningful work in the world. You are a person of strength who has decided to participate in helping those diminished by illness, injury, abuse, or neglect. *You are the Samaritan* who reaches out to help the one ignored by others.

Congratulations and thank you for the life decision you have made, because there is another truth about your work. It is exhausting, sometimes frustrating, and often heartbreaking. The goal of my book *Radical Loving Care: Building the Healing Hospital in America* was to highlight the fact that the American healthcare system is letting you down. It's time for charities to create true environments of Loving Care, to break down the bureaucracies that are crushing your best intentions, and to lift our eyes beyond technology, bureaucracy, and money toward a renewed sense of mission.

Charitable work was founded in traditions that are holy to some and can be seen as sacred to all. The notion of charity arises from the highest expression of love. Charitable work needs to be seen as Sacred Work. Yet it is often done in ways which degrade its meaningfulness. Who are the people that come to charities for help? What stories live behind the faces we see?

If you wonder about whether charitable work must involve sacred commitment, consider the vulnerability of those who come to charities in need. Consider the story of Katrina, a successful client of Nashville's renowned Magdalene program—a sanctuary for those who have been engaged in prostitution and drug abuse. Her story appears at the beginning of a new guidebook prepared by the women of Magdalene so that those trying to establish similar programs around the country can gain a window into the lives of those served.

> *I remember my last days using on the streets. I walked up and down Dickerson Road until a car stopped for me. I got in the car, and the man asked me to have sex with him. I agreed. I then asked him how much money he would give me. He told me how much, and I felt like it was not enough; but I felt compelled to accept his offer because I wanted that next hit of dope so bad. He took me to the park where we had sex in the car. After we*

finished, he dropped me off at the store on the corner of Dickerson Road and Hancock Avenue. I saw the guy who I always bought my drugs from and I bought some dope. I went behind the store to take a hit. I smoked it on a glass stem and tried to forget about what I had just done.

Without the refuge of Magdalene, Katrina might have continued to destroy herself. In the embrace of the loving arms of Magdalene, Katrina has been able to reach back through the layers of dirt and grime and pain in her recent life to rediscover her soul. She has new life not because Magdalene gave her some high-tech treatment to reprogram her brain, but because they offered her the healing power of love.

Why do we need to hear stories like Katrina's? Because, fortunately, most of us don't live lives like hers. She needs us to be able to hear her story so we may identify with her and, in so doing, find in our hearts the compassion she needs from us.

No matter how much their service may include the use of sophisticated technology and utilize complex business strategies, charities are not factories where transactions dominate. With surprising frequency, those who knew I was leading a hospital would say things to me like, "Hey, that's quite a body shop you're running over there!" or, "How are things over there at that expensive hotel you run?"

The subtext beneath these comments suggests that many do not see hospitals or many other charities as places of sacred encounters. Instead, they see them as locations where broken "things" are fixed. A central goal of this work is to explode such myths. If we think of hospitals or other charities in this way, we are demeaning the precious nature of this work. Katrina came to Magdalene at a crossroads in her life. She didn't come to be "fixed" or "reconditioned." She came seeking a grander and more complex thing: healing.

In order for caregivers to heal, they must themselves feel support and caring in their place of work. Leaders need to treat them with a respect that appreciates caregivers as engaged in Sacred Work.

A healthy workplace, like a healthy person, is an organic environment that needs nourishment, not a piece of machinery that needs a little tinkering to make it run. Loving caregiving needs to balance skill, efficiency, and excellence with compassion and kindness.

The purpose of *Sacred Work* is twofold: to lift and intensify our understanding of charitable work as sacred, and to explain how to plant and grow

4

cultures of Loving Care in America's charities. It is the practical guide for the implementation of Radical Loving Care.

Can things change? Absolutely. People, and work cultures, have an endless ability to morph from one kind of setting to another. Most of us think and act differently based upon whether, for example, we are being searched at the airport by a security officer or watching a comedy on television. We act differently at worship services than we do in department stores. And we behave differently if our supervisor is a dictator than we do if our supervisor is kindhearted. It simply means that our personalities are dynamic. We have the capacity to think and act differently depending on the decisions we make and the environment in which we live each day.

Although we can, to a degree, choose how we feel, there are other important determinants that range from brain chemistry and hormonal balance to the way we are treated by others. For the purposes of this book, the most important behavioral determinant is culture.

STEPFORD CAREGIVERS?

The first version of a movie called *The Stepford Wives* (based on Ira Levin's novel) appeared in 1975. The basic story is of a group of men so intent on remaking their wives into their own idea of perfection that they literally allow their wives to be converted to robots—human-looking machines that always smile, always speak politely, and essentially serve as slaves. The movie was popular enough that the phrase Stepford Wife entered the language of popular culture. The movie may be contemporary (and it was remade in 2004), but the idea of trying to force humans into robotic conformity is as old as the Roman Empire and as recent as Nazi Germany. The notion also rears its head in a range of company-sponsored programs designed to create a sort of Orwellian groupthink. Company cultures can, directly or indirectly, compel everyone to dress the same and act the same in an effort to get them to think the way the CEO wants them to.

The premier illustration of this is some military cultures where entering recruits are intentionally "brainwashed" so that they can be reformed into effective fighting machines. It can be difficult to get people to kill other people. That task becomes easier if humanity is suppressed.

A broad look at the design of the so-called customer relations programs increasingly popular in some nonprofits suggests that the goal of such a program is to create Stepford Caregivers—individuals who mechanically repeat scripted language and adopt plastic smiles.

The problem with these programs is not only that they don't work for very long—they also breed cynicism in both employees and clients. The predictable failure of these programs causes vast groups of employees to groan each time management introduces a new consultant who offers the latest bag of tricks to "make the organization more user-friendly."

Programs that seek to address only surface behavior are fundamentally flawed when applied to charitable work. It may be okay for fast-food employees to say: "Welcome to McDonalds, may I help you?" But is that the kind of greeting that would warm the heart of someone like Katrina, seeking to escape prostitution, or a rape victim entering a hospital ER, or a cancer patient arriving for chemotherapy?

Phony surface behaviors suggest phony missions, phony work, and phony vision. They suggest that the center of charitable work is about customer-service tricks, not loving-service skill and compassion. People who are ordered to smile can do so. But human beings have the antennae to know when they're being conned.

Of course it's important to be polite. But effective politeness arises from the wellspring of a loving heart, not from the tainted waters of some customer-service trick.

Alisa Shackelford, R.N., a loving nurse who formerly practiced at Riverside Methodist Hospital in Columbus, now practices nursing at a hospital in Charleston, South Carolina. She understands the power of this work. Alisa doesn't need a script to learn how to be caring. She needs the support of leadership in hiring other loving caregivers to work alongside her and to support all first line staff in the delivery of Loving Care.

Once nurses experience a culture of Loving Care, they never forget it. Sarah Kaminski, R.N., was a nurse at Riverside Methodist Hospital from 1987 to 1991. Before and since, she has worked at several other hospitals from Detroit to the Carolinas. She wrote to me recently: "Most of the nurses and other healthcare workers I know are frustrated, have low morale, and don't even realize how different it could be. When I give them specific examples of how things were so much more positive at Riverside, they have a hard time imagining such a place."

Fortunately, such places exist (some are cited herein), and hundreds more can be created if leaders will open their eyes to the possibilities and their hearts to the power of creating loving cultures of care. Charitable work, to be effective, must grow from loving intent. Charitable organizations must create cultures that nurture this kind of intent.

AS SIMPLE AS ABC

U nderstanding the principle of loving culture is critical to appreciating and embracing the core approach in establishing healing environments. To simplify, imagine that you and the people with whom you work are in one of three categories: A, B, or C.

The A group is made of those who completely embrace the notion of Loving Care. You can tell this not by what they say, but by how they act. These are the ideal caregivers who routinely commit extra effort, who live lives of compassion and excellence, and who are deeply dedicated to the mission of caring. They make up ten to fifteen percent of a given work force.

A-group leaders emphasize partnership, value the ideas of others, tolerate constructive criticism, encourage innovation, affirm the importance of first line staff, and see themselves as servants whose job is to inspire, support, and lead with vision.

A-group leaders believe that work, where we spend so much of our lives, can be a place of joy and fulfillment. It doesn't have to be a place of boredom where we while away time waiting for five o'clock or Friday, or count the years and months until retirement when we can really start living.

A-group leaders create work settings that are magnets for creative, productive, and caring individuals.

The C group is at the other end of the spectrum. These are the cynics, disappointed by life, who grumble and complain while offering minimal efforts to complete their work. These individuals may have the capacity to care. Some may even have a Servant's Heart beating down deep within. But it's buried so deep beneath layers of hostility and disdain that, frankly, they will never join an initiative like Radical Loving Care. In fairness, they may not be true cynics. They may simply have an opposing life view: that employees, like new army recruits, need to be dominated and controlled as much as possible. They may be successful in some settings, but their approach is deadly in an environment where compassion needs to live in

8

balance with skill and clinical excellence.

The C group, like the A, makes up a minority—about fifteen percent of most work forces. C-group leaders are dictatorial and focus heavily on control of their staff. They are distrustful of others' suggestions and are intolerant of diversity and different points of view.

C-group organizations attract people who love conformity, predictability, and the status quo. They may draw some good workers but they keep them only with material incentives like money and extra benefits, or through fear tactics. In C-group charities, employees are either dictators themselves, victims, or drones who "check their hearts in the parking lot" each morning and send the rest of their bodies off to go through the motions.

The key group in all of this is the B group. Individuals in the B group are weatherpeople, constantly wetting their fingers to check the direction of the wind and moving their positions accordingly. Almost all of us have elements of the B group within us. Humans need each other and will often tolerate terrible work environment not only to keep their paychecks, but to avoid being shunned. To be shunned (fired, excluded, laid off) is a terrible and frightening human experience. And there are, of course, financial penalties for being cut from a work force. Accordingly, most people are willing to pretzel-bend their personalities to match a given work culture.

The B group is huge and is characterized by a chameleonlike ability to adapt to the source of power. If the charity is run by an A-style leader, the seventy percent in the middle will either migrate toward a more partnership-style culture or they will leave the organization, voluntarily or through termination. Given time, A-style leaders will create A-style cultures. One part of the B group will migrate quickly toward partnership and trust, and the remaining Bs may eventually join. The C group will be left out in the cold.

In *Radical Loving Care*, I described culture migration as "Wave Theory." Once a strong A-style leader is in place, the Wave (represented by the leading edge of the B group) will begin to shift. Soon the entire temperature of the ocean will warm as the caring waters of A-style approaches take hold.

C-style leaders are just as effective in moving the Wave in their direction and in freezing the waters of culture. The extreme examples of this kind of leader are people like Hitler, Mussolini, and Stalin, who swung millions of ordinary, B-group human beings behind their cruel C positions. We all know organizations or teams that are run by miniature versions of

9

Stalin. They lead by fear and intimidation and the cultures they lead are as cold as their own hearts.

What about B-style leaders? Since the majority of the population is in group B, the percentage of organizations run by B-style leaders is about the same as the percentage of B-groupers in any organization. Most charities, from hospitals to small organizations, are run by bland individuals who operate as managers more than as real leaders. They don't want to make any waves and their organizations are much like stagnant ponds. The goal is to keep everything the same, regardless of what is best for the people served. With enough energy, desire, and understanding, it is possible for a B-style leader to join the ranks of the A leaders.

The ABC Theory is the basis for the action plan in this book. The goal is to create an A-style vision and an A-style culture. It is to utilize and develop A-style leaders to grow cultures that both motivate and, in some cases, replace the work force.

CEO COMMITMENT: THE KEY TO REAL CHANGE

Without the right leadership, the change process is doomed. With the right leader, the work is guaranteed to succeed as long as the leader remains committed.

What steps can A-leaders take to create change? The actions described in this book can work no matter the size of your organization as long as the *intention* is driven by love. If the only reason for initiating a program of Radical Loving Care is to crank up patient satisfaction numbers or because you think this approach will help you beat the competition, then you are thinking transactions instead of love, and the program won't work over the long term. You will ultimately fail, because the idea of Sacred Work is grounded not in transactions but in loving intention.

The single biggest condition necessary for successfully growing a culture of Loving Care is CEO commitment. Can the garden be created without it? It's possible, but very difficult. The work of growing a loving culture is so difficult that CEO resistance may be all the toxin needed to kill the first seedlings.

As captain and chief gardener, the CEO must commit fully to the work. The reason for this is that she or he is the only person empowered with the ability to drive forward the culture of Loving Care across the *entire* organization. Other leaders or individual first line staff members can have an impact on the culture in their area and their influence may even spread a little to nearby departments. But only the CEO and the senior team can really drive genuine organization-wide change.

In my long experience, if this work succeeds, it is because *a loving leader has nurtured it over two or more years.* It takes at least this long for the new culture to become a pattern. And if the work continues beyond a given leader's tenure in office, it is because the culture has become so imbued with belief in the work as sacred that a neutral or negative leader will have

11

trouble tearing it down.

If you are a CEO or other top leader, what's in it for you? Why do this work? The short answer is that there is no other way to achieve real success as the head of a charitable organization. The longer answer is contained in the section "The Successful Results of Love-Based Leadership," pages 23–26.

TO WHOM DO YOU REPORT?

When I ask caregivers this question, they tell me about their boss. This person may be a supervisor, a vice president, a CEO, or a board of trust.

The best answer, though, is that all caregivers report not to their boss, but to their patients and clients.

Embed this thought into your mental model of work: In charitable caregiving, your "boss" is the person you serve. The people you serve, by the way, are *not* customers. They don't come in to buy a shirt or dress, they come to you in deep need. They have cancer, or heart disease, or have come for your help in delivering a baby. They are the raped, the abused, the homeless, the ignored. They are your mothers and brothers and sisters and children. They come to you because they are suffering in body and soul, and they are calling out to you for help. They are the voice of humanity in distress. They are not asking you to fill their shopping bags but to tend to the cry of their hearts. They need service far beyond customer-focused politeness. They need loving service from people who see their work as sacred.

It is time for every caregiver in America to discover what the best ones already know: We are accountable, first and foremost, to the people we serve.

ARE YOU AN A-ORIENTED LEADER?

To find out whether you are an A-leader within the meaning of this work, there are many questions you could ask But the core one is this: Do you believe and practice a leadership style that is love-based or fear-based?

The chart below will help a leader see the contrasts between love-based (A-oriented) cultures and transactional cultures. In each box is a presentation of an underlying motivation, or a belief and attitude that prevails in a culture type. Note the importance of intention and motivation in a Radical Loving Care culture. The motivations for workers in a Transactional culture are external for the most part, while those for members of a love-based culture are largely internal. Which type of culture do you prefer? Which type of culture is yours?

Underlying Cultural Motivations

TRANSACTIONAL CULTURE	RADICAL LOVING CARE CULTURE
This is a MECHANISTIC model imposed by external forces. Mechanistic assumes that employees need external motivation to do the "right thing." Work is done from the outside in.	This is an ORGANIC model that comes from within like an artesian spring and assumes that employees as partners are internally motivated to give Loving Care. Like the artesian spring, this culture is self-renewing. It's about respect, Loving Care, attention to excellence, and finding your joy from the inside out.
It's a job that has to be done to pay the bills.	The job is Sacred Work, a calling—work is meaningful and something that one wants to do.
The bureaucracy is resistant to change, and is a directive/hierarchical environment in which people are made to do the work "the right way."	The caring community is collaborative—it's all about creating meaning and purpose with intention, and coming to work to have a good experience.
Us vs. Them (Adversarial Perspective). One party must win and the other party must lose.	Collaborative Relationships are essential, as we are all children of God—all brothers and sisters.
"Margin over Mission": Profit is more important that living out our beliefs expressed in our mission. If times are tough enough, the mission will be sacrificed for the sake of profit.	Mission is central to who we are and how we are—expressed through hiring, orientation, retention and affirmations, staff reviews, rounding, and other business practices here and in our relationships with each other.
Efficiency is more important than relationship.	Relationship and efficiency are in balance.
Curing is more important than caring.	Caring and curing are in balance.
Patients are "disease states."	Patients are spiritual beings—body and spirit are integrated, not separated.
Illness diminishes the person.	Illness creates vulnerability.
Employees should not make mistakes.	Loving care is for patients and staff alike—it calls us to do the right things.
Mistakes are punished—we want "zero errors."	Mistakes are learning opportunities.
If you can't measure it, it doesn't matter.	The most important things like love are beyond measure, yet love is visible through a touch, a kind word, and silent listening to those enmeshed in pain and fear—making all the difference in the healing process.

13

Leaders control employees like pieces on a chessboard (controlling model). Leaders expect employees to give their all.	Leaders serve servers—they take care of people who take care of people and ask how best they might serve (collaborative model). Partners are encouraged to give Radical Loving Care not only to others but also to self, replenishing self from the internal artesian spring.
There are dual standards for conscious and unconscious patients. It's all about patient satisfaction scores.	There is the same standard of Loving Care for all patients regardless of their conscious or unconscious state. It's all about giving Loving Care.
Fired employees are exiled.	Underperforming partners are terminated with respect.
Hiring focuses on résumé and skills.	Hiring focuses on the whole person.
Orientation is an information dump. Its purpose is to give as much information in as little time as possible to meet requirements.	Orientation is Inspirational, Informational, and Fun so that partners/employees will better remember what is important.
Annual reviews are exclusively quantitative.	Partner reviews evaluate Loving Care behaviors, balancing the quantitative and qualitative.
Being caring is a transaction, which means: "I'll be nice and act caring toward you if you will reciprocate."	Love and Loving Care is unconditional—it is a way of being and doing.
If you want to know what our mission is, read it in the policy manual. The mission is on the wall.	If you want to know what our mission is, watch a partner's next encounter with another caregiver or patient. The mission lives in our hearts and is expressed through our behaviors, words, and deeds.
Vision is the responsibility of leaders, so only the leaders need to know the vision.	Everyone knows the vision and supports it every day.
Employees work for pay.	Partners get paid to do what they love.
We distinguish between direct and indirect caregivers.	Everyone is involved in giving Loving Care to caregivers and patients, thus everyone is a caregiver.
Business is all about competition—and we need to beat the competition!	As a not-for-profit charity, we work for the common good and so collaborate with others who do charitable work.
Employee recognition focuses only on length of service.	Partners are recognized for exceptional performance across a wide spectrum. Innovation is rewarded!

ORGANIC vs. MECHANICAL MODELS

O ne of the best examples of an A-group culture actually exists in the for-profit world. The example is so famous that it's remarkable more organizations haven't copied it. On a recent trip on Southwest Airlines, I asked a flight attendant why she thought her organization was so successful. "We hire for personality and train for skill," she replied quickly. This is what Southwest teaches. It's significant that not only does this statement reflect a core reason for success, but first line staff people understand the statement and can explain it to others.

Imagine that the attendant had given a longer answer: "We hire because the organization is a living thing run by real people and attitude is critical. We train because we are engaged in the serious work of flying commercial jets. We like to have fun because we believe that enjoyable workplaces draw the best people and create the best outcomes. When people are laughing, it enables them to take their work seriously but not themselves."

There are, of course, other reasons for Southwest's success: uniform aircraft (all Boeing 737s), effective discounting, brilliant leadership, a world-class focus on customer service, a great safety record, low incidence of lost luggage, high occurrence of on-time arrivals, profitability. But in one line, that flight attendant has expressed what I believe to be the single biggest reason for Southwest's *continuous* success over decades. They hire for attitude and then focus on training the individual in the Southwest way of doing things.

Southwest is used so commonly as a model of success that it's a wonder that most charitable corporations haven't yet learned from it. Most of the models for organizational change created in the last century emphasize an approach which suggests that organizations are like large machines that need oiling, adjusting, and sometimes a few new parts. At the other

15

extreme are models which are so organic they provide no foundations on which to build.

Charitable organizations are grounded in human service. They are, by definition, established to meet the needs of vulnerable and hurting people. The ideal charitable organization is a blend of compassion and skill, of kindness and effective treatment. The way to determine the right blend is to base *everything* on a vision of Loving Care.

Most charities say they do this but don't do it. Most hospitals have mission statements that emphasize caring, and behaviors that say the vision of the organization has the following priorities: technology first, money second, employees third. If they are university hospitals, they may literally say, as two heads of major research hospitals have told me: "Our priorities are research, teaching, and patient care—*in that order.*"

If the primary goal is technology, then employees become machine operators. As one radiology technologist said to me: "Basically, I'm a button-pusher." If employees have this self-image, what happens to compassion?

If the primary goal is business, then the board will hire a business-oriented CEO and employees rapidly become "units of expense." Again, compassion is shoved to the sidelines. It doesn't necessarily disappear, it simply becomes a random occurrence.

What about the other extreme? If the goal is exclusively compassion, then the organization may hire people who are nice but technically incompetent.

The goal is balance. Southwest Airlines has found this balance. So has Alive Hospice in Nashville; Parrish Medical Center in Titusville, Florida; The Siloam Clinic in Nashville; and St. Charles Hospital in Bend, Oregon. There are others. It's important to understand two things about achieving a Loving Care culture: 1) it can be done, and 2) once the culture of Loving Care is in place, it tends, like an artesian well, to renew itself.

A culture of mediocrity has trouble attracting excellence—and when good people do happen to enter it, they don't stay long. Cultures of low integrity, like WorldCom and Tyco, attracted many people at the top levels who may have started out with good intentions but end up either leaving or corrupted.

ENERGY AND ALIGNMENT UNDER THE ABC THEORY

T he ABC theory recognizes that where attention goes, energy flows. An A-style charity leader directs the attention of the organization toward positive visions of Loving Care and environments of excellence. C-style charity leaders live and act out of fear. They create fear-based cultures because fear keeps the work force distrustful, disorganized (without the leader), and, they hope, at bay.

AS COMPLEX AS ABC—IMPACT ON CLIENTS

What happens when clients enter a C-style organization? They will likely encounter clipboard-style receptionists who make eye contact only to intimidate. They will soon feel like hostages because that's what a control organization wants their clients to be. First and foremost, clients of C-style organizations must *behave.*

Remember, it is possible for good outcomes to occur in a C-style setting to the degree that the subject is engaged in a machine-style transaction. But charitable organizations deal with vastly more complex issues. An abused child can't be healed in a machine. A rape victim won't recover unattended by caring human beings. The dying experience was mishandled so badly by hospitals stuck in mechanical models that hospice programs became a necessity. Even in the case of a broken leg, excellent treatment (as opposed to adequate treatment) requires kind human interaction. What if the person with the broken leg is a field goal kicker or a self-employed sole breadwinner whose injury destroys family income?

ALIGNMENT OF GOALS

On a visit to a giant clinic that serves the poor, I was met at the door by the CEO.

"How's it going?" I asked as we walked down the hall.

"We're having a great day," the CEO answered quickly.

"What does a great day look like?" I inquired.

"Did you see that waiting room? It was full. A full waiting room is a great day for me because we're here to provide care for the poor. The more people that come, the more I know we are providing access to care. People know about us and trust us."

Later, as I headed toward the door, I stopped to talk with a clerk at the front desk. "How's it going?" I asked.

"Not too well," she said.

"What does 'not-too-well' look like?" I asked her.

"It looks like that," she said, pointing at the crowded waiting room. "For me," she continued, "last Friday was great. The waiting room was almost empty."

If I had taken the chance to ask a patient what a great day at the clinic looked like, the person might have said, "I like it when the waiting room is empty because that means I'm going to be seen right away."

Which of these people is right? The answer is that each of them has the response that is true for them. From the standpoint of what's in it for each of them, the answer depends on one's point of view—literally and figuratively. Sacred Work asks the question: "How can we get the CEO and the first line workers on the same page?" Ideally, the front-desk clerk would share the vision of the CEO: *the more people in the waiting room, the more I have the chance to practice my best gifts of serving others.* When the work is seen as sacred, that is the way each first line staff member feels most of the time.

I have seen CEOs try to control the thoughts of partners by telling them what to think. "You are not to think negatively about our new partner hospital," I heard one say to a large group of employees one day. "I expect all of you to be glad about this merger."

What a ridiculous comment, I thought. He thinks people will think differently if he tells them to. Three years later, this same CEO, departing from his job, told his replacement, "I guess I failed at bringing these two big hospitals together." Admirable humility, but it would have been so much better if he had become aware at the beginning of the flaw in his leadership approach and could have accepted the need for another way.

First line staff will not align their thinking with the vision of the CEO simply because he or she *tells* them to, especially if the CEO has created a culture of fear. The best fear-based leadership can ever accomplish is *surface compliance.* Fear-based leadership loves to use weapons like shame, repression, and humiliation to force compliance, but what this creates in most employees is feelings of worthlessness and anxiety. These are great prescriptions for organizational depression and low morale. This approach also breeds suspicion, gossip, and deep mistrust. In the presence of such feelings, it's astonishing that a fear-based leader ever hears a good idea from someone else.

Love-based leadership creates a dialogue that allows the majority of staff to integrate a new way of thinking into their mental models. There will rarely be total alignment, but love-based leadership always has the best chance of winning the full engagement of hearts and minds, because love-based leadership respects the sacredness of each person's thought process.

THE FOUR KEY
ENCOUNTERS

Unfortunately, love and compassion have been omitted from too many spheres of social interaction for too long. Usually confined to family and home, their practice in public life is considered impractical, even naïve. This is tragic.

—The Dalai Lama

The quality of human encounters is an outgrowth of the community culture that exists in each organization. Change the culture, and you change the texture of the encounters that occur within it.

There are four key encounters in any healthcare system:
- Caregiver to Patient (The Primary Encounter)
- Caregiver to Caregiver
- Leader to Caregiver
- Caregiver to Self

Complex emotions and the endless shadings of love can never successfully be reduced to a diagram. Still, I have created a simple model that can be used as a common reference point. Symbols as simple as a Star of David or a Cross or a Crescent and Star signal entire lines of theological and spiritual meaning. I have chosen a modified Venn diagram to symbolize the core notion of encounters.

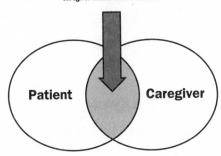

Primary Encounter

This becomes sacred whenever the
caregiver meets need with love.

Patient   Caregiver

The entire objective of Sacred Work is to enrich the primary encounter between caregiver and patient. To make such an encounter meaningful, even sacred, requires that each of the other three kinds of encounters be strong and loving.

In my model, actual encounters between patients and caregivers can be either transactional (functional) or meaningful (loving) in *varying* degrees. The ultimate successful interaction is the one I referred to as the Sacred Encounter in my book *Radical Loving Care: Building the Healing Hospital in America.* This encounter is the hypothetical perfect balance of quality and caring. If the word Sacred carries too much religious baggage for you personally, then substitute the word "meaningful." In every Sacred Encounter, God, as Love, is present. For those who disavow any concept of God yet feel and understand a different energy when they have a meaningful caring encounter, this energy is Love.

On the following page is a diagram which puts the caregiver in the center instead of the usual model that highlights the patient. The purpose of this is to reinforce that the caregiver is the key to successful patient care. The other circles represent some, but not all, of the caregiver's other relationships. The leader's key job is to make sure the caregiver receives care.

Caregiver Relationships

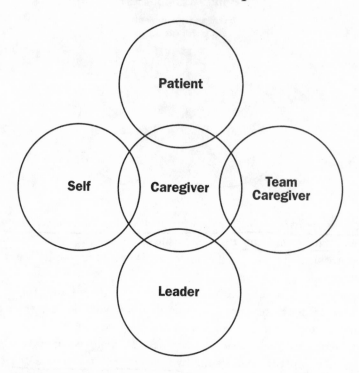

THE NEW GOLD STANDARD—
CONTINUOUS LOVING CARE

Caregivers achieve new levels of excellence when they find balance in each of the key relationships described above. The religious would perhaps envision the key relationship as the one they have with God. If this is critical to you and if you think that the resolution of this issue resolves all others, then that will be your answer to the question of how to make every encounter a loving encounter. In any case, for purposes of organizational thinking, this diagram reinforces the essential role of the leader as caregiver for caregivers. That is how leaders affect first line care of patients. They take care of the people who take care of people.

The heart of success for a hospital or charity is that it offers quality love-based care to everybody all the time. If you accept this as the gold standard, then how can it be achieved? Assuming perfection is impossible, the goal is to come as close as possible.

THE SUCCESSFUL RESULTS OF LOVE-BASED LEADERSHIP

In the culture of our time, big television networks ballyhoo so-called reality television. In 2006, programs like *Survivor* (CBS) and *The Apprentice* (NBC) air each week. A half-step off these shows is ABC's *The Bachelor* and *The Bachelorette*.

The core message of these programs is a Darwinian theory of leadership: that success is about survival of the fittest, that you win by undercutting the other person, and that somehow, Donald Trump and Martha Stewart are the epitome of successful American leadership.

To watch some of the leaders of America's hospitals and charities in action, you would think they subscribe to such notions. I cannot count how many times I have heard leaders of nonprofit organization talk of "killing the competition" and "getting a competitive edge," as if the goal was to destroy other community service entities.

Love-based leadership doesn't instruct us to ignore similar charities. But it does call us to maintain primary emphasis on the mission, and service to those in need. True love-based leadership understands this. Can you imagine Mother Teresa trying to block another charity from serving the poorest of the poor in Calcutta? She welcomed any good help she could get. Her work was not about competing with other orders of nuns or with other denominations. It was about loving service.

- Who would you prefer to model in your charitable work, Donald Trump or Mother Teresa?
- Can you find Martin Luther King's balance of tough-mindedness/tender-heartedness in your work, or are you tilting too far one way or the other?

23

- To what kind of leadership does the mission of your organization call you?

It may surprise some that when the attention of leaders is focused on creating cultures of Loving Care, both quality of care and business outcomes usually improve. This is because love is about more than compassion. Love is also about quality and discipline and efficiency and stewardship. There is nothing loving about a nurse giving a patient the wrong medication or a social worker who makes serious mistakes in discharge forms.

As I wrote in *Radical Loving Care,* my experience as a CEO leading three different hospital systems over a quarter-century, together with my observation of other organizations, proves that positive outcomes flow from loving leadership. In general, these outcomes have included:

- patient satisfaction levels consistently maintained in the 98th percentile.
- reduced employee turnover.
- higher employee satisfaction.
- higher productivity.
- lower absenteeism.
- better financial outcomes.
- stronger clinical quality.

These, of course, are the hallmarks of any successful hospital or charity, and every single one of theses outcomes was recorded over many years at Riverside Methodist Hospital in Columbus and Baptist Hospital System in Nashville. The same has happened at Parrish Medical Center in Florida, St. Charles Hospital in Oregon, and Alive Hospice in Nashville. These outcomes can be achieved, and the culture changed, by attracting the energy of leaders and caregivers to the practices and beliefs that create loving culture.

AWAKENING GENIUS IN THE ORGANIZATION

This question is sometimes raised: Are we trying to train people or simply awaken something within them? The answer is always that it's not one or the other, but both.

Love-based leaders have a fundamental faith in other people. They know that the spark of some kind of genius exists within each person. I'm not talking about genius measurable with typical aptitude tests. I'm addressing the special gifts each person has, gifts that will *never* be offered

24

by people in a fear-based setting but are freely unwrapped in the warmth and trust of love-based environments.

At Baptist Hospital, patient transporter Effie Welch has the genius of a loving heart and a passion to care for others. She makes more of an effort than most leaders I know to actively affirm everyone around her. She sends endless numbers of cards, emails, and handmade notes to her partners, remembering their birthdays, encouraging them with her love and kindness.

Claude Huguley, an assistant chaplain, has the genius of quiet presence. He is one of the shyest people I have ever encountered. Yet he is universally loved for his ability to be present to families in the midst of deep sorrow.

Keith Hagan, M.D., has the genius of a loving heart. He has world-class skills as a urologist. But it is his ability to love his patients that brings about the balance between compassion and technical ability.

Dr. Rhonda Switzer, head of Interfaith Dental Clinic, has the genius of endless energy. Her drive has helped lift her clinic to a top place among healing ministries in this country. Simultaneously, she regularly cares for patients herself!

George Mikitarian, President and CEO of Parrish Medical Center, has many genius abilities. But the one you see first is his warm and engaging smile. As soon as you see it, you know you're going to like him. And good people always do.

Laura Madden, R.N., has the genius of faith. It informs her eyes, lightens her smiles, guides her tears, opens her heart, and creates in her the ability to be one of the top Neonatal Intensive Care nurses anywhere.

Marcy Allton has the genius of organizing energy. During her twenty-five years at Riverside Methodist Hospital, she brightened the lives of thousands of employees by organizing the best recognition events I have ever seen.

Rhonda Swanson has the genius of gracious presence. In her sequential roles assisting a hospital CFO, a hospital CEO, and a hospital Medical Director, she engages the genius of her grace by comforting the often angry and impatient people who "want to see the boss right now." Her particular genius hasn't just staved off lawsuits. It has created positive experiences for people who, before they came to see her, were having negative ones.

Karen York, a vice president at Alive Hospice, has the genius of being able to balance rule-making with kindness and humor. She balances what may look like conflicting simultaneous roles with the grace of a ballerina. Her responsibilities include Human Resources, Loving Mission, and

Compliance Officer. How do you compel compliance with JCAH rules and teach loving mission at the same time? It takes her genius to make it work.

Barbara Quinn, President of the Park Center, a charity which cares for people with significant mental illness, has the genius of being able to tolerate endless interruptions. Instead of sealing patients off from her and hiding behind a locked door, patients literally wander in and out of her office all day long, into the middle of meetings, into the middle of her speeches, into the middle of her life. Through it all, she treats each interrupting person with respect, caring, and compassion. As a result, she has created, in a very difficult environment, a radically loving culture.

There are literally millions more examples of genius around us all the time. The central message is that this genius must be allowed to come alive inside an organization. Genius is a flower that needs nurturing. In the presence of fear-based leadership, these flowers may never bloom or, if they do, may quickly wither and retreat. The challenge of loving leaders is to:
- recognize the presence of the potential for genius in each person.
- awaken its expression.
- renew it with constant encouragement.

PART TWO

The Season of Learning

Essential Tools

TOOLS TO CREATE A LOVING CULTURE

The fifteen tools presented in this section are meant to enhance your understanding of how to rethink your environment. The notion of tools in Sacred Work is to convert concepts to pictures. Each of these tools describes complex concepts in overly simple terms so as to create a common language. Since the work is complex, it's important for us to struggle to create clear symbols so that we can communicate with each other more effectively.

For example, what does balance look like in a loving culture? Below is a picture that uses the literal image of scales. The purpose of this picture is to reinforce the idea that Sacred Work is not only about kindness and compassion. There's nothing loving about being kind but sloppy, being compassionate but unskillful. Martin Luther King's injunction that we be tough-minded and tender-hearted in balance is a superb description of balance in a single phrase.

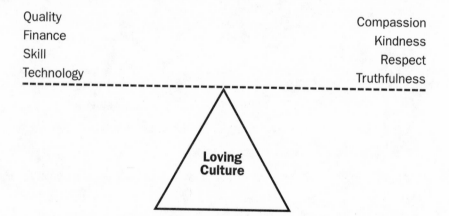

Quality
Finance
Skill
Technology

Compassion
Kindness
Respect
Truthfulness

Loving Culture

In this section are fifteen tools that should help you picture a new culture. Use these tools to implement the programs that are part of Radical Loving Care.

Tool #1
POSITIVE LANGUAGE

G ary Vacca, a former key leader at Lourdes Hospital in Paducah, Kentucky, taught me an important concept about positive leadership. He told me that there are neurolinguistic studies that demonstrate an important fact about negativity. The human brain does poorly at computing the word "No" as an adjective. When people see a sign that says "No Smoking," they immediately think of smoking—the opposite of the goal of the sign. Their cognitive thinking understands that smoking is not allowed, but some other part of their brain, if they are smokers, immediately desires smoking.

Without checking the research, this makes perfect sense to me. It's the reason good coaches never say "Don't miss" to one of their players before a free throw or field goal. Negative words create negative thoughts.

Although the sports world seems to have learned this lesson of leadership psychology, the charitable world appears to have missed it. Nurses are constantly warned against medication errors. "Don't give the wrong medication," or "Let's not have any patient falls," are common instructions. The positive leadership alternatives, the ones more likely to generate good reactions, are like this one: "Let's be sure we're keeping patients as healthy as possible by giving the right medications and looking after their safety."

As the culture of Loving Care is launched, it is important to affirm the good that already exists in the organization. Much better than saying, "We're doing a lousy job and we'd better turn things around" is to say, "We have so many loving people here that we have a great chance of making this an even more loving place."

It takes most leaders lots of conscious practice to convert negative, fear-based language into positive, love-based language. Start the practice now as you begin the first steps of initiating culture change.

ACTION STEPS

- Start listening to your own language and the language of those around you.
- Practice framing things in a positive way. For example—
  Negative: I need to stop being irritable.
  Positive: I am going to focus on showing kindness and grace to others.

Tool # 2
THE PROCESS WHEEL

Cultures of Sacred Work in communities of Loving Care are made up of processes that move in cycles, or seasons. *Doing* is an important process, and most organizations are good at doing. But do they understand and remember why they are doing what they are doing? Stepford Caregiving is mindless doing. Loving support-givers appreciate the reasons for what they are doing, and understand the mission and vision of their organization. Doing is *action*. The hardest season, for those raised in western cultures, is to appreciate the importance of *being*.

All great performers understand, intuitively, the importance of being vs. doing. This idea can be heard in countless quotations from athletic heroes who talk about *being* the baseball, or *being* the hockey puck. Musicians talk about becoming one with their instrument. In caregiving, Mother Teresa set an example of being one with the poor that she served.

The tool before you is a simple picture that shows different zones in the cycle of Sacred Work. Try to keep it in mind as you guide yourself and others through change.

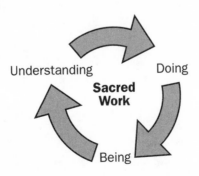

Understanding   Doing
Sacred Work
Being

ACTION STEPS

- Determine if you and your team are in balance by examining the Process Wheel and thinking about the time that is spent in each zone.
- Are you spending too much time in the Doing zone?

Tool # 3
FOUR-PART PATTERN CHANGE

Unloving behavior comes from old ways of thinking. It's necessary to change our patterns of thinking and acting if we truly want to make a habit of loving behavior. This can be difficult, but there is good news: If we are sincere about wanting individual and organizational change, a blueprint is available to us. Psychologists have identified a clear four-phase cognitive change process that is enormously powerful and consistently effective when pursued by organizations as well as by individuals. Determine an area of behavior you would like to change, follow this process, and you *will* change.

Yet pattern change is so difficult that two more things are required: *motivation* and *persistence*. From this point forward, we will use the four-phase process in story after story as a way of imprinting the process.

This is not about tinkering, but real change. It's not just a program, but a phased installation of permanent change. It's encouraging to know at the outset that this process is guaranteed to succeed. The only way it can fail is if we give up.

Phase One: Awareness

Being aware of what needs to change may seem obvious to some, but lack of awareness is the biggest reason necessary changes are not made. Developing realization, perception, and knowledge (awareness) of a situation that requires change is the first step to making that change. Here is a simple example I like to use. Assume you hate Monday mornings. You may simply continue to live in dread of Monday mornings, or you may become *aware* that this attitude is a negative thing in your life.

33

Phase Two: Acceptance

Awareness does not cause change by itself. If you want Monday-hating to depart from your life, you need to accept that it's important enough to focus some of your energy on this. Where attention goes, energy flows. You may need to look into the mirror of the obvious and say, "Hey, there's going to be a Monday every seven days. Why should I allow my life to be darkened every seventh day?" Remember, real change is not about faking new behaviors. It's about discarding old attitudes in favor of new ones.

Phase Three: Integration

If you have now accepted the need for this change, you need to *integrate* the idea into your life. This means you have to imagine a new vision of Monday morning. To do this, you have to ask yourself about current reality. What are the attitudes that are producing toxicity? Why do you hate Mondays? Is it because you don't like your job? Or is it because you have unconsciously gone along with an American culture which has been telling you to hate Mondays and love Fridays? (The restaurant is called TGIF for Thank God It's Friday. There is no restaurant called TGIM to honor Mondays, is there? That very idea makes most people laugh.) What would your thought process look like if you chose to start liking Monday mornings? You don't have to love them. But what if you started to like them?

Phase Four: Action

The Action phase will naturally flow from the Integration phase. If, anxious for action, you jumped over the Integration phase and tried to act, you were probably disappointed. You discovered that it's not enough just to wake up Monday morning and say to the mirror, "Oh great, it's Monday!" These words fall flat as you feel the old Monday dislike tossing its customary poison into your stomach. Pattern change is hard. The patterns of years or decades won't vanish in a single Monday. Typically, we need to really think this through at the Integration stage, try it out, try it again, rethink it, and try again. Eventually, if you choose to like Mondays and succeed, it will mean you have effectively integrated a new and better pattern into your life. You will have recaptured one-seventh of your life and made Monday a more positive experience.

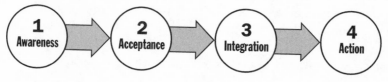

In many of the stories in this book, I will insert the four phases, with the words *italicized,* as a trigger to reinforce the power of the process. Meanwhile, begin applying this process to some aspect of your own life. Pick a negative pattern of your own and use the four-part system to change it. Start with something as easy as the Monday morning example. This will give you practice both understanding and changing things in your work setting, and it will help you begin to integrate this tool into your thinking.

ACTION STEPS

- Write out the four phases of pattern change on an index card you can carry around and start using them.
- Apply the four phases to some problem in your own life.
- Start using the four phases as a thought tool in evaluating change in your work area.

THE SEASON OF LEARNING

Tool # 4
THE FIRELIGHT WINDOW

O ne of the most important culture drivers in any organization is the process of hiring, counseling, and reviewing staff members. I have adapted a tool for use in this process called the Firelight Window (also described in *Radical Loving Care*). This tool has become essential to support leaders seeking a method for evaluating and supporting staff members during the change process. In a love-based culture, this tool works both ways: partners evaluate leaders as well as the reverse.

The Servant's Heart & The Firelight Window

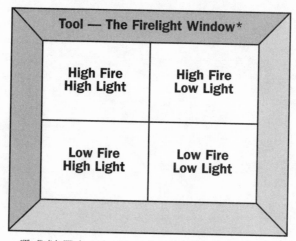

Tool — The Firelight Window*	
High Fire High Light	High Fire Low Light
Low Fire High Light	Low Fire Low Light

*The Firelight Window is adapted, in part, from a model developed in leadership training at General Electric Corporation on evaluating staff around results and values.

36

The Firelight Window is a tool of fundamental value in building a Healing Hospital. When it comes to hiring, orienting, reviewing, and firing, this window is a key guide. It has been used in a different form at General Electric, and it can help leaders in their regular efforts to both develop and review staff performance. We should be looking for strong performance (fire) as well as strong values (light).

I. Top Left Quadrant: Great Performance and Great Values (High Fire, High Light)

The core of a Healing Hospital emphasizes both performance outcomes and values. Ideally, a Healing Hospital is populated by staff members who balance great values with great performance. These are the partners who routinely demonstrate an ability to achieve excellent results with high integrity. These are the dream employees everyone wants to have. In a Healing Hospital, a conscious and sustained effort is made to support and retain these partners. In fact, when I have encountered partners in this category who threaten to leave for another job or retire, I usually pull out all the stops to try to retain them. Great employees attract other great employees, and their departure should never be taken lightly. In a Healing Hospital, the job may be replaceable, but *no person is replaceable* because each person is valued as unique.

II. Lower Left Quadrant: Kind but Ineffective (Low Fire, High Light)

Partners in the lower left quadrant are characterized as people who have lovely values in general. They are the kind of people you would love to have as friends or dinner partners. The problem is that they *seem* to lack the fire to generate good results in their current role. It is quite likely that people in this quadrant may seem to lack fire because they are simply in the wrong position — and may be with the wrong organization. The goal in the improvement plan is to see if that fire can be awakened in their current role. If not, the kindest thing for all concerned is to attempt to guide these people toward settings where their passion may be ignited.

III. Top Right Quadrant: Effective, but Unkind or Unfair (High Fire, Low Light)

We often see partners who achieve what appear to be strong results. On further examination we find they have gotten these results in spite of displaying poor values.

THE SEASON OF LEARNING

A classic example of this is the surgeon who is the owner of both talented hands and a terrible temper. Quite often during the past three decades a nurse has come to me with the complaint that a particular surgeon has lost his temper, shouted at the staff, and thrown his instruments. Over my years as a hospital CEO, when I would inquire further about constructive discipline in cases like this, the usual response would be something like: "Well, Joe has a bad temper, but he's a great doctor." In a Healing Hospital, *there is no such thing as a great doctor who treats others with disrespect.* Otherwise good doctors or nurses with anger problems need to be directed to anger management counseling..

IV. Lower Right Quadrant: "Self-Firers" and "Radar Dodgers" (Low Fire, Low Light)

The lower right quadrant is made up of a group I typically refer to, somewhat flippantly perhaps, as "self-firing." What's unfortunate is how long many of these partners will hang around an organization. Some of them have developed a particular skill I call "radar dodging."

Every large organization seems to have a few of these — they are people who are both ineffective and not very well motivated, yet no one ever seems to get around to letting them go. They seem to have an instinct for how to fade into the woodwork whenever there's a layoff and will often outlast partners who are far more useful to the organization. Radar dodgers cannot dodge effectively in a Healing Hospital.

The key to dealing with partners in the top right or lower left quadrant of the Firelight Window is a pattern of three to six months of leadership counseling to attempt to move these partners over into the desired top left category. This counseling is done through a review process.

ACTION STEPS

- Practice using the Firelight Window by describing it to a colleague and discussing how you might apply it to yourself.
- Recommend the use of the Window to the Human Resources Department.
- Whether the organizaiton adopts it or not, use it yourself as you evaluate yourself and the work of others.

TOOL # 5
SENGE'S ICEBERG EXPANDED

Peter Senge, renowned author of *The Fifth Discipline*, uses the model of an iceberg to illustrate that what we see of almost any issue or work situation is "the tip of the iceberg," and that what is truly important is what is going on below the surface, where most of the iceberg lies. The Iceberg Theory, as applied by me here, suggests that most of what is important in human relationships (and thus, the culture of an organization) goes on beneath the surface. The problem is that most leaders seek to make change by engaging in customer service programs which only touch behaviors visible at the tip of the iceberg. Because they have not tackled deeper change below the water line, they make no meaningful alteration in culture.

ACTION STEPS

- Tinkering *vs.* Tackling: To what degree is your organization, team, or department simply tinkering with problems instead of tackling them?
- To what degree are you simply tinkering as opposed to tackling issues below the surface?
- Can your own courage lead you to explore below the surface and discover deeper answers to the issues of Loving Care in your life?

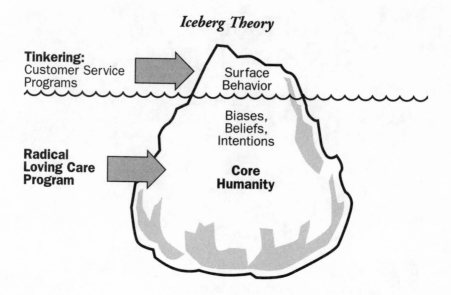

TOOL # 6
TRACKING QUESTIONNAIRES AND APPRECIATIVE INQUIRY

M ost organizations use questionnaires in one way or another to test attitudes and to gauge the mood of both employees and patients. Such questionnaires can be helpful in creating Sacred Work if careful attention is paid to the kinds of questions that are asked, and if questionnaires are used in a spirit of what my long-time friend and colleague Tracy Wimberly, drawing on the wisdom of academicians at Case Western's Weatherhead School, calls a process of *Appreciative Inquiry*. More than just cross-examination, Appreciative Inquiry includes a careful, honest, and probing look at the beliefs and behaviors in an organization.

Where attention goes, energy flows, and questionnaires move and direct energy. If employee reviews focus entirely on whether nurses are completing their charts and showing up promptly for work, that is where the energy will flow. If the review process is more balanced and includes the expression of kindness, respect, and compassion in work, the energy will find a better equilibrium.

Questionnaires of the kind we use through our Healing Trust work are excellent tools to gauge baseline attitudes and to help organizations develop a picture of the degree to which they are love-based or fear-based. These instruments can signal a new sensitivity to issues that may never before have been considered.

The use of questionnaires is an excellent way to engage large numbers of people in the new work of the organization. Fear-based leaders like to make the decisions themselves. Love-based leaders like to engage the

41

opinions of others. For example, Brian Lee's Custom Learning organization does a wonderful job of engaging first line staff in high-energy work.

We can learn what an organization thinks is important by paying attention to the questions asked by the organization. Questions are important signals to board members as well. If the predominant questions of trustees have to do with financial performance, what does that say about caring mission?

LEADER QUESTIONNAIRE

1. **Loving Care means:**
    a. touchy-feely stuff.
    b. a way to raise our patient satisfaction scores.
    c. always being kind.
    d. delivering good customer service.
    e. the best balance of compassion, clinical excellence, and financial stewardship.
    f. a name for the latest flavor-of-the-month program .
    g. the truest expression of our mission.
    h. all of the above.
    i. e. & g. above.

2. **On a scale of 1 to 5, with 1 being Very Low Priority and 5 being Top Priority, what is the current importance of Loving Care in our organization?**
    1 = Very Low Priority, 2 = Low Priority, 3 = Medium Priority,
    4 = High Priority, 5 = Top Priority

3. **On a scale of 1 to 5, with 1 being Strongly Fear-Based and 5 being Strongly Love-Based, how would I describe our organizational culture?**
    1 = Strongly Fear-based, 2 = Fear-based, 3 = Neutral,
    4 = Love-based, 5 = Strongly Love-based

4. **Our board fully understands the Loving Care initiative as described in Radical Loving Care and Sacred Work.**
    1 = Strongly Disagree, 2 = Disagree, 3 = Neutral, 4 = Agree,
    5 = Strongly Agree

www.healinghospital.org

5. **Our board fully supports the loving care initiative.**
   1 = Strongly Disagree, 2 = Disagree, 3 = Neutral, 4 = Agree,
   5 = Strongly Agree

6. **On a scale of 1 to 5, with 1 being Strongly Opposed and 5 being Fully Supportive, rate your personal feelings about a three-year initial commitment to establishing a stronger love-based culture.**
   1 = Strongly Opposed, 2 = Somewhat Opposed, 3 = Neutral,
   4 = Somewhat Supportive, 5 = Fully Supportive

7. **On a scale of 1 to 5, with 1 being Strongly Disagree and 5 being Strongly Agree, rate the following statements as they concern your organization:**
   a. If we make a three-year commitment to this work, we can significantly improve our organization through creating a love-based culture. _____
   b. Most of our medical staff actively practice a love-based approach in their practice of medicine. _____
   c. Most of our first line caregivers practice a love-based approach in their delivery of care. _____
   d. I am satisfied with the level of our patient satisfaction. _____
   e. I am satisfied with the level of our partner/employee satisfaction.

   _____

8. **The biggest challenge we face in succeeding with this work is:**
   _____
   _____
   _____

9. **The best thing we have going for us in succeeding with this work is:**
   _____
   _____
   _____

THE SEASON OF LEARNING

BOARD QUESTIONNAIRE

Rate the following statements as they concern your organization:
1. As a board member, I believe the single most important element of our mission is the delivery of Loving Care.
    1 = Strongly Disagree, 2 = Disagree, 3 = Neutral, 4 = Agree,
    5 = Strongly Agree

2. I believe that our mission calls us to think of our work as sacred or deeply meaningful.
    1 = Strongly Disagree, 2 = Disagree, 3 = Neutral, 4 = Agree,
    5 = Strongly Agree

3. I would like to see the organization make a full commitment to the development of a deep and rich culture of Loving Care.
    1 = Strongly Disagree, 2 = Disagree, 3 = Neutral, 4 = Agree,
    5 = Strongly Agree

4. If we had a richer culture of Loving Care, our patients and all of our staff would benefit.
    1 = Strongly Disagree, 2 = Disagree, 3 = Neutral, 4 = Agree,
    5 = Strongly Agree

5. The board should establish a committee to support leadership in its campaign to grow a culture of Loving Care.
    1 = Strongly Disagree, 2 = Disagree, 3 = Neutral, 4 = Agree,
    5 = Strongly Agree

The biggest challenge we face in establishing a culture of Loving Care is:_____
_____
_____
_____

The biggest advantage we have in establishing a culture of Loving Care is:_____
_____
_____
_____

PHYSICIAN QUESTIONNAIRE

Rate the following statements:

1. My practice of medicine is grounded in Loving Care (a balance of skill and compassion), and this fact expresses itself in most of my dealings.
   1 = Strongly Disagree, 2 = Disagree, 3 = Neutral, 4 = Agree,
   5 = Strongly Agree

2. My colleagues regularly practice Loving Care.
   1 = Strongly Disagree, 2 = Disagree, 3 = Neutral, 4 = Agree,
   5 = Strongly Agree

3. I could benefit from further education on how best to practice Loving Care in my work
   1 = Strongly Disagree, 2 = Disagree, 3 = Neutral, 4 = Agree,
   5 = Strongly Agree

4. My colleagues would benefit from further education on the practice of Loving Care
   1 = Strongly Disagree, 2 = Disagree, 3 = Neutral, 4 = Agree,
   5 = Strongly Agree

5. I support the efforts of leadership in growing a culture of Loving Care throughout the organization.
   1 = Strongly Disagree, 2 = Disagree, 3 = Neutral, 4 = Agree,
   5 = Strongly Agree

6. Loving Care is the centerpiece of our work.
   1 = Strongly Disagree, 2 = Disagree, 3 = Neutral, 4 = Agree,
   5 = Strongly Agree

The biggest challenge we face in establishing a culture of Loving Care is:_____
_____

The biggest advantage we have in establishing a culture of Loving Care is:_____
_____
_____

THE SEASON OF LEARNING

45

EMPLOYEE QUESTIONNAIRE

Circle a number from 1 to 5 under each statement.

1. Loving Care means the equal balance of skill and compassion.
   1 = Strongly Disagree, 2 = Disagree, 3 = Neutral, 4 = Agree,
   5 = Strongly Agree

2. I practice Loving Care regularly in my work.
   1 = Strongly Disagree, 2 = Disagree, 3 = Neutral, 4 = Agree,
   5 = Strongly Agree

3. My colleagues practice Loving Care regularly in their work.
   1 = Strongly Disagree, 2 = Disagree, 3 = Neutral, 4 = Agree,
   5 = Strongly Agree

4. My supervisor is a good example of Loving Care.
   1 = Strongly Disagree, 2 = Disagree, 3 = Neutral, 4 = Agree,
   5 = Strongly Agree

5. The top leadership are good examples of Loving Care.
   1 = Strongly Disagree, 2 = Disagree, 3 = Neutral, 4 = Agree,
   5 = Strongly Agree

6. The culture in this organization is primarily fear-based.
   1 = Strongly Disagree, 2 = Disagree, 3 = Neutral, 4 = Agree,
   5 = Strongly Agree

7. What is the current importance of Loving Care in our organization?
   1 = Of No Importance, 2 = Of Little Importance, 3 = Somewhat
   Important, 4 = Important, 5 = Very Important

8. The culture of this organization is primarily love-based.
   1 = Strongly Disagree, 2 = Disagree, 3 = Neutral, 4 = Agree,
   5 = Strongly Agree

9. I spend lots of time worried about the security of my job.
   1 = Strongly Disagree, 2 = Disagree, 3 = Neutral, 4 = Agree,
   5 = Strongly Agree

10. Compassion can sometimes be expressed in a few seconds.
    1 = Strongly Disagree, 2 = Disagree, 3 = Neutral, 4 = Agree,
    5 = Strongly Agree

11. My supervisor leads primarily by fear and intimidation.
    1 = Strongly Disagree, 2 = Disagree, 3 = Neutral, 4 = Agree,
    5 = Strongly Agree

12. The only way to express Loving Care is if you have lots of time to give it.
    1 = Strongly Disagree, 2 = Disagree, 3 = Neutral, 4 = Agree,
    5 = Strongly Agree

13. I know fellow workers who have the ability to express Loving Care just by the way they are present.
    1 = Strongly Disagree, 2 = Disagree, 3 = Neutral, 4 = Agree,
    5 = Strongly Agree

14. Most of my fellow workers dislike their jobs.
    1 = Strongly Disagree, 2 = Disagree, 3 = Neutral, 4 = Agree,
    5 = Strongly Agree

15. The main responsibility for organizational success rests with leadership.
    1 = Strongly Disagree, 2 = Disagree, 3 = Neutral, 4 = Agree,
    5 = Strongly Agree

16. Most of my fellow workers love their jobs.
    1 = Strongly Disagree, 2 = Disagree, 3 = Neutral, 4 = Agree,
    5 = Strongly Agree

17. I play a significant part in the success of this organization.
    1 = Strongly Disagree, 2 = Disagree, 3 = Neutral, 4 = Agree,
    5 = Strongly Agree

18. This organization has a deep commitment to mission.
    1 = Strongly Disagree, 2 = Disagree, 3 = Neutral, 4 = Agree,
    5 = Strongly Agree

19. In today's environment, I don't have time to give Loving Care.
    1 = Strongly Disagree, 2 = Disagree, 3 = Neutral, 4 = Agree,
    5 = Strongly Agree

20. I love coming to work each day.
    1 = Strongly Disagree, 2 = Disagree, 3 = Neutral, 4 = Agree,
    5 = Strongly Agree

THE SEASON OF LEARNING

POWER TOOL: SPECIAL WRITING/INTERVIEWS/TEACHING

Questionnaires are valuable, but meaningful Appreciative Inquiry for all groups can also challenge them to put their own thoughts about Loving Care into words. This works best when we provide individuals with the chance to *teach* others their thoughts about Loving Care. We may not be sure what we think until we have to teach it, and teaching someone else is often the way we learn the best.

Ask others to describe to you what they think about Loving Care.

- Ask them to speak their thoughts. In a circle, ask each person to say one way they show Loving Care. Go around the room again and ask each person for a second and a third way, so long as the exercise seems productive. You can make this a weekly exercise in which one or more staff members give an example of how they expressed Loving Care that week. Every time you ask this question or use this exercise, you are directing energy toward Loving Care and raising the loving energy of the group.
- Ask each person to write a single page that describes three ways they express Loving Care in their work.
- Ask each person to tell a story about when they have been a recipient of Loving Care and what it meant to them.
- Ask each person to tell how and from whom they learned about Loving Care.
- Ask each person to describe things they do to sustain their energy to give Loving Care.
- Ask staff members to identify ways they would like to improve and what changes in thought are needed to accomplish this change.

You can use thoughts gained from the above exercises to create a staff devotional or opening thought to share with the group. This can be done in an approach called *Huddles,* which is recommended by both the Ritz-Carlton Hotels and the Studer Group, a healthcare management development company. Huddles are five-minute meetings (always done standing up) during which members of a work team gather in a circle. One member reads a one- or two-minute story or essay that focuses on a single theme. In this case, the theme would be some subset of Loving Care such as a moment of unconditional love expressed in caregiving. The rest of the team then offers brief comments, and the huddle ends with a phrase everyone says together like: "Live Love."

ACTION STEPS

- Hand out the questionnaires to people in each group and ask them to fill them out.
- Take the questionnaire that fits you.
- See if you can guess how other groups would respond to each question.
- Review the results carefully and in context with other data.
- Make use of the Power Tool (Special Writing/Interviews/ Teaching) described above.

THE SEASON OF LEARNING

TOOL # 7
WAVE THEORY

The Wave Theory is useful for leaders who want to understand just how culture change happens. Imagine your organization is divided into groups A, B, and C. The A and C groups represent the opposite ends of the spectrum, with A being leaders of Loving Care and C the fear-based leaders and cynics. Remember that the big crowd is in the middle.

The goal is to develop the Loving Care approach so that it rises in the organization like a wave, slowly, steadily, powerfully. As the wave rises, it moves the majority in the right direction. Remember that *you never need 100% support* to establish a culture of Loving Care. Once the wave begins to rise, the culture, like the water, like momentum, will shift.

Wave Theory® in Visionary Change

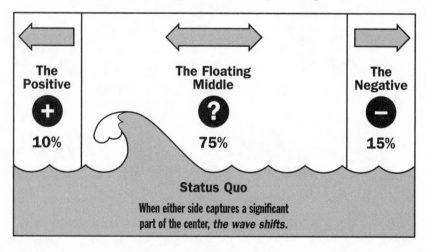

ACTION STEPS

- Where is your team/department/organization on this chart right now? Are you more toward A or more toward C?
- Using the diagram, explain to someone else how the Wave Theory can apply to your team or department.

Tool # 8
MAGIC THEORY

ix years ago, my four-year-old grandnephew, Kyle Sawyer, taught me the basis of Magic Theory. After pretending to withdraw a coin from the back of his ear, I reversed the age-old trick and asked, "Kyle, how did you make that coin come out of your ear?"

I had reversed the age-old trick by suggesting to him that it wasn't my magic that produced the coin but his. I tell this story often to audiences and they are rarely able to guess Kyle's response. His answer to me was: "I don't know how I made the coin come out. *I just did it.*"

Subsequently, I tried the trick on dozens of other four-year-olds. I even videotaped ten of them to demonstrate the predictability of responses from that age group. Time after time, they answered the same way Kyle did.

Adults smile at the story but often miss its application to loving leadership. From Kyle's story I developed a question I used to ask caregivers at Baptist Hospital all the time: "How do you give Loving Care?" They often begin by answering the same way Kyle did: "I don't know. I just do it." But they followed that response with beautiful examples of exactly what they do. "I try to distract people from the pain of the moment and make people smile," Kim, a phlebotomist, told me one day. "I try to make sure I am listening for what they need from me," Deadre Hall, a neuro-intensive care nurse told me. "Maybe they need for me to be cheerful. Maybe they need for me to cry with them. My job is to be a blessing to them."

Magic Theory is all about asking the questions that release potential. Caregivers already possess all the magic powers they need. It is the job of leaders to help awaken this power by *asking the right questions* and listening respectfully to the answers.

Some caregivers tell me, "I don't have time to give Loving Care." How much time does it take to have a healing encounter? In *Radical Loving Care*

I told the story of Lois Powers, the Baptist Hospital cashier who practiced healing by telling jokes to people who passed by her each day.

Nurse Laura Madden practices healing touch by laying her hands on the backs and bellies of the tiny babies she cares for. Lorraine Eaton expresses Loving Care with the eye contact she makes with her critically ill patients.

There is magic in all of this. It doesn't have to take a lot of time to give very powerful doses of Loving Care. Although it's nice to have lots of time to give Loving Care, we all know the magic ability of so many people to help us feel better in a matter of moments—through the tone of their voices, the touch of their hands, the way they enter a room, the way their eyes engage us.

Remember: The magic tool available to every caregiver and leader is the tool of asking questions that assume the wisdom of others and then listening respectfully to the answers.

Many children grow up with strong images of angels and dragons. It's not difficult to spot the dragons of adult living. Some of them occupy the other cars in rush hour traffic. Some wear the uniforms of supervisors. Many haunt news reports on television and computer screens. Some occupy the organizations we politely call competitors. Sadly, the very people we serve in our work may sometimes look to us like dragons.

Where are the angels to save us from all these threats? Where is the magic?

The adult form of magical thinking is called love. Wisdom can enable us to think differently about the difficult people in our lives. The demon in the other car in rush hour traffic is another human being like us— scared, alone, anxious, and yes, loving. The fire-breathing supervisor has within his or her heart the ability to change from a dragon into an angel or at least a normal human being (unlikely as that may sound as you envision this person).

Other organizations are not evil competitors but groups of people trying, as we do, to succeed in their work. And if the people we serve seem like dragons, we are in the wrong work. People wounded by life are vulnerable and in need of our help. We can ignore them, demean them, or serve them with Samaritan love.

What magic do I see at work? I am flooded with images of it in Middle Tennessee as well as in hospitals around the country—caring hands at Alive Hospice that wrap themselves around patients and shepherd them with love up the last mountain of life; a community of angels at the Magdalene

53

charity who spread their wings, rescue women from the two-headed dragons of drugs and prostitution, and hold them in the sanctuary of their loving arms; a circle of saints at Siloam Clinic whose hearts are so large they can encircle the sick and injured of over a hundred countries; a society of magicians at Interfaith Dental Clinic who perform the special trick each day of handing out brand-new smiles to people once afraid to laugh for fear of exposing their teeth.

At a place called First Steps, small beings with incurable illness are healed by love each day by people who give the gifts of their hearts. On the third floor of Baptist Hospital, specially trained hands deliver breath to some of the smallest lungs in the world. At the Campus for Human Development, the homeless find dignity once again in the respectful eyes of loving servants. Troubled teens wandering the desert of dangerous streets may think they see a mirage when they encounter the warm family of a place aptly named Oasis. While at McKendree Village, caregivers deliver love to some of the earth's older beings.

At Vanderbilt Children's Hospital, Belmont School of Nursing, and Meharry Medical College, professors are teaching students the healing gift of Loving Care. The results of their wisdom and compassion will ripple out from each caregiver and into the lives of countless patients. Those patients will know, whether or not they recover physical health, that they have received the healing gift of love from the heart of a stranger, a Samaritan come to tend to their wounds.

In Titusville, Florida, healing is delivered to patients at Parrish Medical Center by caregivers committed to delivering this gift. They are led by the enlightened CEO George Mikitarian, who succeeds because he believes in the genius of his staff to give love.

These are the gifts of magic that live each day and night in the world. They are there for each of us to see, hear, experience. And we can, if we choose, become a part of this miracle by supporting it, by recognizing its existence, by putting our faith into practice through the magic of our love.

One of the differences between childhood and adult magic is that the adult version requires lots of understanding and effort. Children believe naturally. Adults must relearn belief. Children naturally trust. Adults have felt the dagger of betrayal too often to move easily into the land of hope. Small children know nothing about fake behavior. Adults have learned to wear many different masks.

Sacred Work is demanding. But it is the only work worth doing in our lifetime. Is there any better way to live than with love?

ACTION STEPS

These are the key questions for you to ask others and yourself:
• How do you practice Loving Care?
• How have you expressed love today?
• How do you practice love towards the "unlovable" people in your life?

Tool # 9
STORY CATCHING

In the telling of their stories, strangers befriend not only their host but also their own past.

—Henri Nouwen, *Reaching Out:*
The Three Movements of the Spiritual Life

O nce charitable work is understood as sacred, stories appear everywhere. They were always there, of course, but the previous culture may not have noticed. This book is laced with stories because stories are a great way of creating awareness and hope. Stories trigger pattern changes because they provide us with the chance to draw our own conclusions. When the conclusions we draw are our own, they hold greater power than conclusions in the form of dry instruction about how to behave that we may have heard from a teacher.

Stories give us hope. If someone else can do it, so can we.

Stories give us new ideas. They allow us to transfer learning from one setting to another.

Every organization should have a way of catching stories and spreading them. It is through the stories we tell that we learn about our culture and signal the values by which we live. It is also the way we can establish *a new culture.*

Loving cultures always use stories as tools to transmit mission from person to person. Stories are essential to the growth of loving culture.

As Nouwen teaches, listening respectfully to stories from patients or clients are ways we can create warm, safe, and sacred places for the wounded to heal. Rape victims who feel unable to tell their stories safely may stay silent, storing poison within. Battered children begin to heal by telling their stories to counselors within a garden of trust. Patients scared of doctors or worried their doctor is in a hurry may withhold important information.

Deep listening is the kind of art practiced by every good physician, nurse, social worker, and therapist. It is through deep listening that the healer learns where to focus his or her best energies.

Loving caregiving creates a safe place for the other person to enter. Stories are a powerful tool to open that space and to celebrate it.

ACTION STEPS

Where attention goes, energy flows:
- Tell stories of Loving Care.
- Find ways to catch the stories of other caregivers.

Tool # 10
THE MOTHER TEST

s hard as *awareness* of the imbalance around Loving Care may be, it is even harder to accept that the challenge of correcting this imbalance is important enough for us to prioritize it as *the single most important thing for us to change*. Like any tough challenge, it's easy for us to state our awareness so long as we don't have to accept the challenge of changing it! We're like the person who is aware he's drinking way too much but doesn't accept that he's an alcoholic and has to create a new lifestyle. Acceptance means the recognition of the need to change. That's more than many are willing to face. The lure of the comfort zone of the status quo remains seductive.

In both the awareness and acceptance stage, it is important to conduct what Tracy Wimberly calls a process of *Appreciative Inquiry* (see page 41). The reality test for anyone interested in the truth about the organization he or she leads comes with tracking typical patients or clients through the system he or she oversees. Carry a copy of the mission/vision statement along on this tracking tour. How are people being treated at every point in the system? How is the morale of the staff? How satisfied are the patients who are using your organization? How committed are other leaders? If your vision is to live a work life where you and those around you are living at the standard of the Samaritan, where each person is reaching out to help and every person is going beyond the typical to the exceptional, then you will surely accept the need for change.

A great way to understand how to *integrate* what you learn is to apply something I call The Mother Test. Remember, integration is about starting to picture what a solution would look like.

If your mother or someone else were being cared for in the system you lead, would you feel confident they would receive Loving Care *without your intervention?* In every hospital I have led, I have received countless phone calls from people who want me to intervene in advance to make sure their loved one receives good care. A typical inquiry is, "My sister is coming in as a patient, Erie. Would you make sure she gets good care?" I understand that anyone entering any one of America's hospitals is scared. A hospital admission typically means there's a serious problem of some kind. Yet people aren't calling me about medical care. They know I'm not a doctor. They want me to be sure their loved one is treated with kindness and respect. They call me because they know about hospitals—kindness and respect is a hit-or-miss proposition!

The Mother Test: Would you trust your co-workers to give Loving Care to your mother (or other loved one) if she came to your organization?

ACTION STEPS

- With a copy of the mission statement at hand, go on a tracking tour of your organization to learn how people are being treated at every point in the system, and to learn about staff morale and leadership commitment.
- Use The Mother Test question often. Ask it of yourself and use it in conversations with others.

Tool # 11
THE CAREGIVING MOBILE

A mobile is a fascinating image of balance. Touch one piece and all the others *must* move.

When one member of a family is ill, the whole family is affected. When one caregiver is sick or grieving, it shakes the balance of the entire team. When a leader verbally abuses a staff member, either individually or in front of others, it sends a tremble through the organization.

There is another truth about mobiles. Once a piece is disturbed, the others will begin to shake and, simultaneously, they will all begin to seek to regain balance. Team members may have individually different ideas of balance, but the team has its own idea of balance. A healthy team will shake when any member is hurt, celebrate any member's joy, and automatically return to a level of balance that has each person in a position roughly equivalent to the one they had before.

An unhealthy team starts out unbalanced. It may or may not respond to the troubles of others. In any case, since it has no positive balance position, it is always out of synchronization. Teams like this make mistakes, chronically underperform, and frequently try to correct problems by blaming each other.

The Caregiving Mobile is a powerful tool in illustrating both the phenomenon of the way illness affects families and the way team members affect each other's lives.

www.healinghospital.org

The Concept of The Family Care Mobile

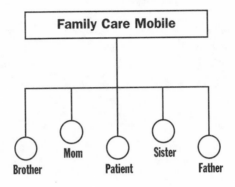

ACTION STEPS

- Make a diagram of the Caregiving Mobile (or copy this one).
- Take as many opportunities as you can to tell other people what it means. Each time you tell others about it, you will understand this concept better.

Tool # 12
SENGE'S VISION/ CURRENT REALITY TOOL

Peter Senge describes the challenge of vision with a simple but powerful diagram that asks us to imagine a rubber band between vision and the way things are at the moment. The higher the vision, the tighter the rubber band. If you want to eliminate all tension, just lower the vision and the rubber band will eventually go slack. If we were to draw the vision of "status quo leaders," Vision and Current Reality would occupy the same space. The value of Senge's image is that it helps leaders understand that they must lead in the area of tension. The vision must be appealing enough to enable followers to tolerate the discomfort of tension.

The Montgomery Bus Boycott went on not for days or weeks, but for months and months (over a year). During this time of great tension, one way Martin Luther King sustained the energy of followers was to continue to remind them of the nobility of their vision.

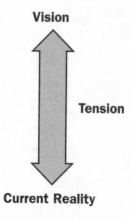

Vision

Tension

Current Reality

ACTION STEPS

- Using the diagram, explain it to someone else.
- What is an example of your own vision and your current reality?
- How can you more effectively deal with the tension in the middle?

Tool # 13
OUR ATTITUDE ZONES

One of the ways caregivers may describe their work lives is by the predominant feeling they have most of the time. Are they mostly bored or mostly panicked? Do they feel comfortable and complacent or challenged?

Many employees describe high anxiety, if not panic, on the first day of work. Fearful of doing the wrong thing or making a bad impression, they study their colleagues for signals. They seek the comfort of routine and may move from anxiety through challenge to comfort as quickly as they can.

We all move through these zones at one time or another. In caring organizations seeking to improve for the benefit of their clients, the Challenge Zone is the only choice. Exciting visions challenge our creativity. It doesn't mean we won't drift up against panic or seek occasional comfort. It means that our predominant energy will circle in the zone of challenge and discovery.

The Challenge Zone is where progress is made and care is improved. The test for leaders is the degree to which staff feel not only challenged, but inspired to succeed.

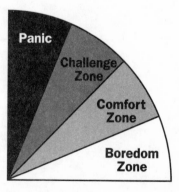

ACTION STEPS

- In which zone are you and your team spending most of their time?
- How can you direct energy to the Challenge Zone?

Tool # 14
THIRD CHOICE THINKING

Third Choice thinking is the best way to avoid getting caught in the tyranny of alternatives that often confront us. Others often want us to pick black or white, yes or no, right or left, when the best choice may be a third alternative or a fourth, fifth, or sixth. Without Third Choice thinking we may feel ourselves trapped into making one of two artificially created choices. With it, we can create alternatives which may well be far superior.

Imagine you have twin children aged eight. They come to you and one of them asks, "Who do you love best, Bobby or me?"

Every good parent knows that the best choice is not to pick one or the other. The Third Choice says to find another answer to the trap of alternatives in front of you. The third and best choice may be something like: "You are both special to me in different and wonderful ways. As your mother (or father), I love you both the same."

There are endless puzzles, practices, and games that caregivers can engage in an effort to gain a new perspective on their work. These practices help us to find the third, or better, choice. The Third Choice tool is a way of challenging staff—to use an overused phrase—to "think outside the box."

Don't allow yourself to be forced into a tyranny of just two options. Create a third and better choice. This is what President Kennedy did in the Cuban Missile Crisis in 1962. Then–Soviet Union President Nikita Khrushchev had ordered his ships to sail through an American blockade of Cuba. Kennedy demanded that the Communist ships turn back. Khrushchev sent a telegram agreeing to withdraw. Before Kennedy could celebrate or respond, a second telegram arrived in which Khrushchev said he had changed his mind and he was refusing to withdraw the ships.

Limited thinking would have forced Kennedy into a tyranny of only two alternatives: Either I order our ships to repel the Soviet advance, risking war, or I order my ships to retreat, risking national humiliation.

Most of the President's advisors immediately fell into this trap of thinking. They began to advise either a tough stand or a retreat. Finally (and thankfully), the President's brother, then Attorney General Bobby Kennedy is reported to have stepped forward with a great example of Third Choice thinking. "Why do we have to respond to the second letter?" he asked. "Why don't we simply respond to the first letter—tell Khrushchev we appreciate his great wisdom in agreeing to withdraw his ships and averting a war—appeal to his best instincts—ignore the second letter."

As history reports, the strategy worked, and there is a good possibility a world nuclear war was averted. At the time, I was a college student. I remember the tension in the room as friends of mine and I watched the drama unfold, wondering if we were about to get drafted out of college and sent into war. I didn't know anything at the time about the decision process unfolding in the White House. All I remember was the collective sigh of relief when the news came forward that the Soviet ships had turned around and were headed away.

We are presented with opportunities for Third Choice thinking all the time. Games allow us to practice this thinking in less-threatening circumstances. Just as looking at a tree in different kinds of light and from different angles helps us to gain a sense of its beauty, games can open our eyes to new ways to both appreciate and solve the challenges before us.

Two of the best games I've seen at exposing elements of culture and thinking are one that I invented and one that I learned from leadership expert trainer Bob Anderson.

THE 10 GAME

I developed this game out of a story I heard from David Whyte about a consultant friend of his who felt compelled to give a fake answer to a client because that's what he thought the client needed to hear. The goal of the game is to test the openness, courage, and honesty in an organization.

Imagine that your boss enters a meeting room where you are sitting with a group of your peers. "Good morning to all of you," he or she says. "I want to show you a new idea of mine. I'm very proud of this idea and

I'm sure you'll love it too. In fact, I think this is the best idea I've ever had. On a scale of 1 to 10, I think this is a clear 10. But I want you to tell me, on a scale of 1 to 10, what *you* think."

Imagine that as soon as you see the idea you think to yourself, "This is one of the worst ideas I've ever seen. I would rank it a 1. I think that if we implement this idea, it might even do some damage to the company."

The boss starts around the room. There are three people ahead of you, and you breathe a sigh of relief. Since you're not first, you're going to get a little time to think about how to speak the truth in a diplomatic way.

The boss calls first on Bob. "What do you think of my great idea, Bob?" To your dismay, Bob says, "Wow, that's a 10, sir. I agree with you."

You know Bob and you know he's just apple-polishing. But it works for him because the boss says, "Great answer, Bob. You know I'll be looking at promotions and bonuses next week and with insight like yours, I think you're in line for both."

Then the boss calls on Judy. "Sure, boss," Judy says shakily. "It looks like a 9 or 10 to me."

"What?" the boss shouts. "You mean you think this might only be a 9?"

"Well, I meant to just say 10, sir. Yes. It's a 10."

"Thank you, Judy. Good answer. You're almost as insightful as Bob."

Next the boss calls on Dave, who is sitting next to you. Dave squirms in his chair. "Well, boss, I can see some advantages and maybe some areas that might need some work."

The boss's face darkens. "What do you mean work? Bob and Judy and I already can see that this idea is a perfect 10, Dave. Do you disagree with them?"

You are praying that Dave will stand his ground. But the crossfire is withering. You begin thinking about your $100,000 salary, your $200,000 mortgage, your wife, and your two teenaged children.

"I want a number, Dave. Give me a number between 1 and 10." The boss is clearly angry. You can sense Dave sweating.

"Okay, sir, I'll tell you the truth. I think it's maybe a 6 or a 7."

"Dave," the boss says somberly, "I'm very disappointed in you. In fact, I'm not sure you are going to have a future with this company. In addition to promotions and bonuses, next week I'll be reviewing which of this team I need to let go. You've just moved to the top of my termination list."

You're next. What would you do? Remember, the truth is that you think the idea is a 1. The boss has now made it clear that if you speak this truth, you're likely to get fired.

Some people with whom I've played this game—especially college students who have not had much experience in the world of organizations—think this hypothetical is a little outlandish. Veteran employees know that versions of this game play out every day. You don't actually need to leave home to encounter this kind of pressure. What if your partner asks your opinion of his or her hair after a visit to the hair stylist? You're thinking it looks terrible. In this case your risk is not your job future and probably not even the future of the relationship. The biggest risk is usually of a brief case of hurt feelings.

In the 10 Game, I have made the stakes higher.

In solving this challenge, it is crucial to remember Third Choice thinking. In spite of my description of it, the majority of people presented with the above problem quickly fall into the tyranny of alternatives. They see their choice as to agree with the boss or get fired.

Some people try to dodge the choice the way Dave did by not answering directly. For the purposes of this game, you have to assume that that exit door is closed to you. The question becomes, can you tell the truth and not get fired? The only way to solve this challenge is with Third Choice thinking. What is the third choice here?

I am tempted to leave this question open so you will have the benefit of learning by coming up with the answer yourself. I'm not sure if the answer I have to offer to you is the absolute best, but I think I've come up with one comes close to preserving both your integrity and your job. Consider these options.

First Choice: "I agree with you, boss. This is a 10." An amazing number of people default to this option right away. They justify it on the grounds of saving their job, their home, their family, whatever. It's not my place to say they're wrong, but I do know that every time you fold up in a situation like this, a piece of your integrity (or soul) breaks off and floats down the river away from you. After a while, your self-esteem collapses as you see yourself as vulnerable to the whims of a tyrannical boss. This kind of thinking is part of what led to recent scandals including Enron, Worldcom, Tyco, and Health South. Everybody kept saying "10" to their bosses when the truth was clearly "1."

Second Choice: "Boss, the truth is, I think this is a 1 and I think implementing it may damage the company." Self-destruction may seem like a marvelous thing when done on behalf of a good cause. In fact, martyrdom has its place. I admire anyone with the courage to speak the truth in the face of the sure knowledge of being fired and exiled from the company and

69

shunned from the group they may have liked working with. Indeed, this second choice takes maximum courage. But it may not represent maximum wisdom.

To determine a better, third choice, ask yourself a key question: Why is the boss trying to force everyone's agreement? In the way I've presented the story, the driving force here appears to be the boss's ego. If this is the case, how might you construct an answer which tells the truth without attacking the boss's sensitive ego? In asking you to think about this, I am not recommending that you keep working for such a tyrant. In fact, I would encourage you to find another job as quickly as possible.

Henry Ford told the truth often enough in his first job at Detroit Edison that he got fired. After Ford's booming success, he thought back gratefully on his firing. If he hadn't been cut loose, he might never have founded Ford Motor Company. In gratitude, he sent the first Lincoln off the assembly line as a gift to the man who fired him.

I hope that at this moment you will stop reading, put this book down, and think about how you would solve this challenge. Training yourself to stay with questions like this is the foundation of learning how to think more creatively. Thinking differently is critical to the success of growing cultures of Loving Care where work is seen as sacred.

Third Choice: "Gee, boss, I must be missing something here. You and Bob and Judy are all saying 10. I haven't been able to see 10 yet. I guess I must be overlooking something the three of you are seeing because I'm only seeing a 1."

Okay, this may not be a perfect answer, but most people in most audiences to which I offer this answer think it has the best chance of preserving integrity and job at the same time. Why? Because my proposed answer makes no criticism of the boss and therefore makes *no attack on his ego.* Instead, I take the responsibility entirely on myself. At a minimum, I am buying myself a little more time to think. At worst, I'll follow Dave out the door to the unemployment office. But I think the worst case is very unlikely.

Are there better choices? Probably. Feel free to email them, or any other thoughts you may have, to me at erie.chapman@healinghospital.org. Meanwhile, the main point is to learn to practice Third Choice thinking. And remember that, like President Kennedy, you don't always have to think up the third choice yourself. You may be lucky enough to have a Bobby Kennedy thinker nearby who will come up with the third choice for you. Be wise enough to take it.

70

THE NAIL PUZZLE

The best leadership puzzle I ever saw about teaching creative problem-solving was one taught to me by leadership trainer Bob Anderson of Toledo, Ohio. When this puzzle is done in a team setting, or even alone, it will demonstrate to reflective people every basic principle that leaders and caregivers confront when they are faced with what look like insurmountable odds. The core challenge is to balance a dozen ten-penny nails on the head of one vertical nail stuck in a block of wood. The Nail Puzzle needs to be a guided experience rather than one learned from a book.

The most important thing to know about puzzles like this is that they are not about how to balance nails but how to deal with seemingly impossible situations. Yet in spite of this, I have seen dozens of groups pass off the Nail Puzzle experience as "just a game."

The Nail Puzzle, like any other meaningful challenge, is a remarkably powerful way to embrace the complexities of problem-solving—first as theory, then as metaphor, then as a work application. At a theoretical level, here are the principles and skills needed to solve any impossible seeming problem.

Understand the problem. What is the issue? In as clear and simple a way as possible, state the challenge to be solved.

Visualize the solution. Picture what the problem would look like if it were solved. Use drawings, word images, anything to help the team "see" a solution.

Have fun. The puzzle poses a problem which automatically creates tension. Tension can block creative cognitive thinking and drain energy from the solution. Tension may produce negative energy with statements like: "This is impossible!" A light-hearted approach serves to ease this tension. This is why successful teams often report that "we had fun working on this problem."

Listen carefully to the team's ideas. It's even worth appointing someone to write down the word images people come up with and to have this same person sketch pictures of possible solutions. By reducing things to two dimensions, sketches may provide alternative solutions not tied to the hard-edged wood and nails.

Encourage each other. I have seen many teams literally give up on this puzzle. These teams always include someone who keeps saying, "This is a trick. It can't be done. This is ridiculous. Let's give up." It will always be tempting to give up rather than to deal with the frustrations of any hard problem. Teams solve problems when they are actively encouraging each other, even when they are feeling discouraged.

Practice courage and persistence. The heart of successful problem-solving is not brilliance, but persistence. The temptation to quit is enormous.

Stay purpose-driven. The mission of the group is about more than solving the puzzle. It is about teams and individuals overcoming hard problems. The puzzle is a metaphor for life. Stay with the problem and work to solve it, and it will teach you and your team skills that are certain to serve your organization well.

In our consulting work, we regularly use problems like the Nail Puzzle to help groups break through the inertia and paralysis of status quo thinking. If you really want to know what it feels like to think outside the box, this exercise is unmatched. It you would like more details on the Nail Puzzle, engage Bob Anderson's group or contact us at the Baptist Healing Trust.

ACTION STEPS

- Integrate Third Choice thinking into your life. You will have chances to do this every day as long as you remember to ask: What other choices do I have?
- Play the Ten Game.
- Play the Nail Puzzle.

Tool #15
HUMOR

The Season of Learning

We need to always take our work seriously, but not ourselves.
—Bobby Kennedy

Since charities are, by definition, dealing with grim and challenging situations, there is a dangerous tendency for caregivers and their leaders to start taking themselves seriously as well as their work. Leadership can set the tone here. Everybody doesn't have to be a comedian, but it's good to identify those who are and encourage them to entertain the rest of the group.

Is humor really a tool? It is in Loving Care organizations. And it's usually a part of every successful team. We call it a tool here because appropriate humor needs to be honed and developed as an integral part of workplace culture.

The world-class leader in integrating humor into the workplace is not Disney, whom you would expect, but an organization that is engaged in very dangerous work. It's Southwest Airlines, of course.

One of the easiest places to use the humor tool is in orientation. Another place can be in partner/employee recognition events. A third choice is at partner picnics and talent shows. A fourth place is in meetings. On some occasions, instead of having people open with a serious devotional, have them open with something funny—a personal story, a joke they've heard somewhere, a reading from Mark Twain or Steve Martin.

Take a look at the use of humor in your organization. Identify the people who have good senses of humor. Encourage them to bring it out. Remember, you don't need to be a standup comic. You need to be yourself. If you're taking yourself too seriously, use this tool to lighten up.

ACTION STEPS

- Look at yourself in the mirror in the morning and laugh. (This may be easier for some than others...)
- Associate more with at least one other person who makes you laugh.
- Encourage respectful joking on your team.
- Find humor around you in places other than TV sitcoms.

PART THREE

The Season of Doing

Concept to Practice

By the numbers:

THE PRACTICE OF LOVING CARE: CREATING EXPERIENCES

It is not the *concept* of love that troubles us. It is the *practice* that challenges our days and nights. Conscientious caregivers and leaders around the country are increasingly seeking help as they confront questions like: How do I give love to a patient who is shouting in my face? How do I practice kindness in the Emergency Department to the fiftieth person that has asked me the question I have already heard fifty times from forty-nine other people? How do I remain patient in the presence of the drug addict in front of me who has relapsed for the fourth time? How do I lead with love and respect in the face of pressures to meet bottom-line money goals pushed upon me by a board that seems to care more about margin than mission?

It is helpful to think of charitable work as creating experiences for everyone involved rather than simply marching through a pattern of transactions. Keep in mind that the goal is not only to complete tasks. Leaders in loving cultures seek to enrich each encounter, to move from fixing to the deeper concept of healing.

Focusing on charitable work as sacred and meaningful will help millions of American caregivers and their leaders live out the love in which all of us believe. Caregiving is noble work when it is practiced with love and dreary labor when love is absent.

I am often asked if there are metrics to measure Loving Care. There are some *outcomes* that can be tied circumstantially to the institution of a loving culture. But the process of providing conclusive proof of the power of Loving Care is exactly as difficult as proofs for the existence of God. How *much* do you love God? How much do you love your spouse or partner or children or parents or friends? And yet, is anything more important?

What we do know is that certain steps are likely, even certain, to lead to a successful journey into the garden of Loving Care. We also know that the establishment of loving culture is an indicator of a successful organization. Loving organizations always succeed because love itself is the only true sign of meaningful achievement.

The order of the steps set forth in this section is not precise. Not everyone travels the journey to success in the same pattern, and you may wish to follow a different alignment of phases. Yet the essential elements are contained in following these processes.

Step One

ASSESS TOP LEADERSHIP COMMITMENT

I n the initial assessment phase, top leadership commits to a covenant for change. The ideal scenario is for the CEO to assemble the senior leadership team for an *awareness* check of current reality and an evaluation of the readiness of the organization for genuine change. Using the tool of Four-Part Pattern Change (page 33), the challenge is to determine if all constituencies are ready to *accept* Loving Care as a core priority of vision. The tools and steps described in this book are ways of creating awareness and acceptance. They also provide ideas on how to help organizations visualize the *integration* of the concept of charitable work as sacred. How will work change when it is seen as sacred? What will thought and behavior patterns be compared to what they are now?

Fear-based leaders like to get their subordinates to parrot the company line. They follow the guidance of the bumper sticker that says: "Beatings will continue until morale improves." Of course, morale never does improve.

Love-based leaders seek to help each person find his or her own voice in the expression of a new vision. This is a process of Appreciative Inquiry (see page 41). The CEO's goal is not to impose a new vision but to elicit genuine feelings and ideas on the role of Loving Care. The new initiative works best if each leader finds her or his own way to articulate a vision of Loving Care that can develop and become unified with input from other partners.

Once the CEO and her or his team have decided to use Loving Care as the guiding principle for a new vision, it's time to engage all other constituencies. Board commitment must proceed hand-in-hand with

THE SEASON OF DOING

77

leadership's vision. A Board Committee can be established to provide oversight and support for the Loving Care mission. In the case of hospitals, do the same thing with the medical staff. (More detail on these two tasks will follow).

ORGANIZATION-WIDE STEERING COMMITTEE

The wisest configuration is to establish an organization-wide Steering Committee that includes board members, physicians, top leadership, and one or more representatives of the first line employee group. The CEO *must* be a part of this organization-wide Committee to signal the deep commitment of the organization.

When this has been achieved, the organization-wide Steering Committee can begin to think about subcommittees. In a wire diagram, the organization-wide Steering Committee would be at the top with each subcommittee hanging below it. There should be a subcommittee, or team, for each of the areas touching culture change—these are the Target Teams I will describe in Step Four. The Steering Committee can provide reports to the board as well as to the organization at large.

Clear vision *for culture change* is important because hope is important. There is no hope without vision and no vision without a belief, created by the leader, that, together, a better culture can and will be created. Few people have the energy to commit to change unless they can drink from the well of a hopeful vision. Enormous energy is released in the presence of a clear and powerful vision as people discover, through the work of a good leader, that the vision is not only exciting but it can be achieved.

The Steering Committee can begin its work by creating two pictures. The first picture should portray the *current reality* of your organization around loving culture. We can call this a **Current Reality Check.** Use the Appreciative Inquiry approach. Check some of the facts around issues like these:

- Is care patient/client-centered?
- Is leadership employee-centered? Are leaders committed to caring for caregivers?
- How is patient satisfaction?
- What is partner/employee morale?
- What is partner/employee turnover?
- How strong is the organization's quality of care? Where are its strengths?

- What is the organization's reputation in the community and beyond?
- Is the organization safe for the users?
- Is the organization financially stable?
- How is staff productivity?
- How committed are leaders and staff? Are they passionate about mission or just going through the motions?

The second picture should portray your *current vision*. This is the **Vision Check.** What does success look like around the parameters described in the questions above? Find a way to describe vision *in just a few words*. You may be surprised to realize how all great missions and movements can, in fact, be described in a few words. For example, the vision of the American Civil Rights movement under Dr. Martin Luther King was *to integrate the South*. There were, of course, the tools of that movement: the use of the network of black churches, nonviolent resistance including sit-ins, lawsuits, lobbying Congress, securing favorable news coverage.

The vision of the NASA's Apollo Space Program was to land an American on the moon. The vision of Disney is to create the best in family entertainment. Southwest Airlines? To create a low-cost, reliable flying experience in a fun environment.

What is your vision? Make your vision statement as bold, inspiring, clear, and specific as possible. Not just "We want to be a better hospital," but "We seek to create a loving culture of service" or "We seek to be a caring ministry devoted to healing with love." The vision should be something any first line partner/employee would be comfortable repeating in the same way that everyone on the front lines of the Civil Rights movement could say, without hesitation, "Our vision is to integrate the South!"

Where was the energy and inspiration behind the vision to integrate? It came from looking at the terrible reality of the times—toxic patterns of segregation and mistreatment of minorities and deciding to do something about it. Remember, everyone in the country was *aware* of the injustice concentrated primarily in the South. Some Americans in the 1950s, but perhaps not even a majority, *accepted* that something needed to be done about it. But many did not. There was the inertia of the status quo, the fear of disrupting it, and the lack of a meaningful vision to change the status quo. Accordingly, no meaningful action was taking place—in part because no significant group had yet pictured (the *integration* step) how to make the change take place.

Vision becomes inspiring as people take a hard look at current reality and decide that:

- things need to change for excellence to be achieved.
- successful caring organizations are built on loving cultures.
- first line staff is going to be part of the change.
- a plan supported by top leaders is underway to make it happen.

BOARD ENGAGEMENT

Perhaps the two most important functions of a board of trust are to set policy and to oversee the selection (or removal) of the CEO and his or her successor. But a board of trust has another key role in the building of a loving-care culture: the board members must engage with this work—understand it, encourage it, offer their wisdom to it, and oversee it.

Current Reality Check: The following are some key checks for evaluating board thinking.

- What is the board's current policy direction? Presumably, it includes some typically vague statements about commission to mission and ensuring the overall delivery of high-quality, cost-effective patient care.
- Does the board consider that it sits in governance over an organization involved in Sacred Work? Or do its members subconsciously think of themselves as financial overseers of a huge body shop?
- Does the board hold the CEO accountable for regular reports on the organization's progress in meeting mission?

I am astounded at what a poor job many boards do in the CEO selection and removal process and how little attention they pay to succession planning. Far too often boards of trust, made up of volunteers, stick with the comfort of minimal effort and status quo leadership. Search firms are rarely challenged by board search committees to find leaders who have the ability to inspire and enlighten. Instead, questions often circle around a potential CEO's ability to "manage problems" and, of course, to generate a good bottom line. I know this because I've served on numerous boards and I've been through several CEO searches. I've also seen boards of trust remove outstanding, innovative leaders and replace them with drones selected because "they won't rock the boat." There is nothing wrong with seeking skills of problem management and effective financial performance. But these skills should be an outgrowth of strong loving leadership, not its centerpiece.

Vision Check: Establish a Board Steering Committee or standing committee that will: 1) develop an understanding of Sacred Work and the role of the Radical Loving Care initiative, and 2) receive reports from the organization-wide Steering Committee and other committees. As the overall governing body, the board does not need to be engaged in day-to-day decision making. But culture change requires support at all levels, and the vision of Radical Loving Care sits at the center of mission and drives vision. Therefore, board engagement is important.

Establishing board involvement in the Loving Care initiative can very well have another good outcome. As the board members become immersed in the value of loving leadership, there is a good chance they will become wiser in dealing with both policymaking and long-term issues of CEO succession.

SPECIAL SECTION FOR HOSPITALS: FOCUS ON MEDICAL STAFF

In a hospital, a parallel assessment/covenant effort should be launched with the physicians on the medical staff. Although the initial energy in many organizations may aim toward influencing partner/employee morale and participation, the medical staff needs to be engaged in a parallel initiative. For CEOs considering how to begin this work, the key principle to keep in mind is *guided self-determination*. This means there will be guidance and encouragement from administration, but the primary energy to back change must flow from medical staff leaders. Physicians must frame this work in language that they find effective for them, keeping carefully in mind that we are talking about love, compassion, and balance, not about superficial customer service tricks.

Step One. *Identify key physicians* who demonstrate sensitivity concerning the role of compassion in medicine and the balance it plays with technical skills.

Step Two. Engage top medical staff leadership, including the Chief of Staff, in appointing a Physician Steering Committee whose assignment is to determine the appropriate role of Loving Care in medical practice at your hospital. Be sure this committee fully understands the work that employee groups are doing. Make sure the chair of the Physician Steering Committee is made a member of the organization-wide Steering Committee.

THE SEASON OF DOING

Step Three. Challenge the Physician Steering Committee to *look at the key culture drivers* of medical staff culture. (A list of organization-wide culture drivers can be found on page 90.) For example, Privileging is analogous to Hiring.

Privileging

Current Reality Check: What is the process for privileging? Does the privileging process make any effort to evaluate the physician's commitment to Loving Care?

Vision Check: If the work of the organization is precious and sacred, privileging would require interviews and background checks of potential physician staff to determine their support for and receptivity to an environment of Loving Care. Doctors may be surprised to come across a hospital that is paying attention to such things. And they should also be impressed by it. What if the signal to new physicians is that your organization is not just another hospital, that it subscribes to the notion of work as sacred, and that physicians will need to come on board? After all, can you imagine wanting a physician on your staff who says, "No, I don't want to be any part of an organization that lives out a culture of Loving Care." If you get an answer like that, why would you want such a physician on your staff?

Loving Behaviors

Current Reality Check: Is there currently any initiative by the medical staff to advance or support Loving Care in the hospital?

Vision Check: Ask the Physician Steering Committee to appoint a Physician Subcommittee to actively identify speakers for Grand Rounds who can address subjects like compassion in medicine. Massachusetts General Hospital does this on a regular basis. At Riverside Methodist Hospital in Columbus, Ohio, an annual award (which I set up and funded) is given to a physician based on his or her display of compassion with patients and staff. Along with the award is presented a lecture on compassion. The whole process is overseen by Dr. Pam Jelly-Boyers who, as Director of Medical Education, actively works to advance the values of Loving Care through both residency training and medical staff education. What if your hospital initiated such efforts?

Physician Support for First Line Staff

Current Reality Check: How do doctors treat first line staff (and vice versa)? What happens if a doctor is abusive toward staff?

Vision Check: What could be done to raise awareness among doctors of the importance of caring behaviors toward staff? Most hospitals have physician appreciation programs. What about a program in which physicians are encouraged to express appreciation for first line staff? Where attention goes, energy flows. What would happen if physician recognition of staff were advanced through some kind of event in which physicians were called upon to speak about their particular gratitude toward individuals or teams of caregivers?

Caring for Caregivers

Current Reality Check: Is anything being done in your organization to look after the health of caregivers and to address the widespread problem of compassion fatigue?

Vision Check: Establish a physician group that will attack this challenge directly. Under the encouragement of Drs. Keith Hagan, Roy Elam, Liz Krueger, and Cheryl Fassler, all highly regarded physicians, an initiative has been developed in Tennessee to offer physicians pathways for healing to help them deal with burnout and avoid the traps of impairment. It is important to note that the goal of this initiative is not to deal with already impaired physicians, but to help those who are healthy to stay healthy. The core approach is aimed at using Rachel Remen's Meaning in Medicine approach to help doctors regain balance in their work. What could your organization do to help caregivers find healing and respite so they can be at their best for the patients and colleagues who depend so deeply on their help?

THE SEASON OF DOING

STEP TWO
LAUNCH THE RADICAL LOVING CARE CAMPAIGN

When leaders are ready to commit to the Loving Care initiative, it's time for an organization-wide launch of the effort. This means rally-type speeches from top leaders and others announcing the initiative. Whether the organization is as small as five employees or as large as thousands, this kind of public commitment helps signal a new day in the organization.

The only downside to launching a campaign is the instant feeling that will live in the hearts of many that this will be another "flavor-of-the-month" program. Two things should demonstrate that this is not true. The first is time. Over the passage of time, staff will see if a new day is truly dawning or if leadership isn't able to sustain their commitment. The second is that true loving care can never be just another new program. Sacred Work is at the *center* of caring. To abandon the idea suggests the organization has died to its mission. To embrace it signals that leadership is committed to embracing and enriching the organization's mission and vision and that they truly seek to live its best values.

If the initiative is launched using an outside speaker like someone from the Baptist Healing Trust, it is critical that in-house staff be prepared to articulate and carry forward the essence of the work after the outside speaker leaves. Outside consultants and speakers can be inspiring, but they don't live every day in the organization. Everyday leaders and everyday staff are the ones who must embrace this work.

Increasingly, I like to use campaign-style materials—buttons and badges and wrist bracelets and posters (made by the staff or by an outside agency). There is always the risk that energy will rise and fall, so the campaign must have many phases. Loving Care is in the nature of an article of faith and is as important as core beliefs. In the Jewish religion, the Star of David is an eternal symbol, not something that comes and goes. The same is true of the cross of Christianity.

For people of all nationalities, flags are important. For Loving Care, it is important to find enduring images. I use the intersecting circles of a Venn diagram to symbolize Sacred Encounters. This is an easy image to reproduce and the symbol becomes a reminder of the sacred importance of meeting each need with love.

Primary Encounter

This becomes sacred whenever the
caregiver meets need with love.

Lance Armstrong and his organization have reached millions of Americans with the use of a simple yellow bracelet that promotes a way of life. "Live Strong," the plastic bracelets say. In 2005, the bracelets popped up on wrists from California to Boston to Paris to Tokyo.

The Trust plans to support a similar program with dark-red bracelets that will probably say something like: *Live Love*. It doesn't matter very much whether you use bracelets or lapel pins or posters or all of the above. In the Wuesthoff Hospital System along the Space Coast of Florida, Senior Vice President Johnette Gindling got the staff to create a series of gold pins. The goal was to give two pins to each person as a way of recognizing them for some aspect of Loving Care. That person would in turn give one of the pins to someone else for the same thing. Simultaneously, Loving Care has been woven into the goals of each individual leader.

The *Sacred Work* video we made at Baptist Hospital is a marvelous way to enhance the campaign, and its effect should last for several years. It shows the staff in action ministering to patients, and it is powerful because it is true. It is so effective that more than one hundred hospitals nationwide are using it. This kind of documentary video is a powerful way of saying to the organization: *This is what we look like when we're doing our best work. Let's do this all the time.* And it's a wonderful way to honor the powerful nature of the work of the organization.

Campaigns can include the initiation of new practices. At Alive Hospice, Vice President Karen York decided to launch followup phone calls to the families of patients two to three weeks after the patient experience had ended. This turned out to be a beautiful way for staff to surprise families with the sense of an ongoing commitment to their welfare.

At Nashville Baptist Hospital, an organization-wide quilt was created to represent different aspects of Loving Care. The quilt was set up on a sort of loom in the lobby of the hospital. Over a period of several months, all partner/employees were invited to sew something into the loom. Whether it was a single thread or a whole patch, this was a fantastic way to engage the organization. And imagine what visitors thought as they learned from staff members the purpose of the quilt.

The point is to engage the organization in the effort through the energy of a campaign. This approach can be just as effective with a small organization.

The more ways the Loving Care initiative can be made visible in the organization, the more the staff and its clients will test leadership on the sincerity of the initiative. This is good. Every challenge should be taken by leaders as an opportunity to deepen commitment to the effort and to expand understanding.

The frequent use of committees in this work is merely an example of the degree to which active teams can bring wisdom to the effort and how committees provide continuous opportunities for participation.

REVISIT VISION THROUGH A VISION COMMITTEE

fter top leaders have completed their assessment of vision and current reality, a Vision Committee should be established. This team must have the full blessing and active support and engagement of the CEO and other top leaders, and it is best if the CEO actively participates on the committee, though not necessarily as chair. Remember, the CEO has already articulated a vision that can serve as the foundation of future development. The role of the Vision Committee is to coordinate the organization-wide initiative that will grow the seeds of Loving Care.

No matter what your vision is, it's time to revisit and refresh the meaning of caring work. The Vision Committee should be established for vision alone. Its membership should be diverse, drawing from all departments of the organization. The goals are multiple.

Clarity. Frame a mission *everyone can understand.* Mother Teresa understood this in a vision statement that not only motivated her order of nuns but inspired the world: "We will care for the poorest of the poor." And her order understood that the target group were the so-called untouchables in the back streets of Calcutta. Notice she did not say, "We will make all the poor rich" or "We will eliminate poverty."

Inspiration. Make sure the vision is challenging enough to be *inspiring* yet not so remote as to be unachievable. There's no point in writing a vision that says, "We will generate world peace." Nice as that sounds, it's so lofty and unachievable that it's not likely to energize anyone. The vision of the Civil Rights movement is a lovely illustration of inspiration coupled with challenge: "We will integrate the South." Again, the statement didn't say, "We will integrate the world," or "We will make everyone love everyone else."

Buy-in. Secure *buy-in* by engaging as many stakeholders as possible in the vision process. At Baptist, we took a year to develop our mission statement. By the time we were done, over a thousand stakeholders had participated in the process.

Beginning. Start doing the work before the vision statement is complete. Although the final language may be important, the internal work of establishing a culture of Loving Care should begin while the vision work is proceeding.

Dynamism. Vision statements are dynamic and should never be viewed as "finished." The problem with mission and vision statements that are viewed as "complete" is that they end up being framed and forgotten, invisible on the walls as employees wander by never noticing. This is the reason that first line employees (not to mention managers) can rarely recite anything close to the content of the rambling documents that paper the walls of most hospitals and charities. On the other hand, partners at truly successful organizations like Southwest Airlines or Disney can not only tell you the vision but they recite it with a passion that says they truly cherish the work.

ESTABLISH A STEERING COMMITTEE FOR CULTURE CHANGE

M erge the Vision Committee into the organization-wide Steering Committee as shown in the diagram below. This can be called the Steering Committee for Culture Change. The first work of the committee is to evaluate vision and determine a list of *culture drivers* that need to be affected in order to generate change. For example, a culture circle should be assigned to look at Hiring, because the way new staff is hired affects culture. Bring in negative new employees and they will pour poison into the work culture every day. These kinds of employees are the weeds that damage the garden of Loving Care, and they need to be kept out. When they get in, they need to be either converted to the cause or removed.

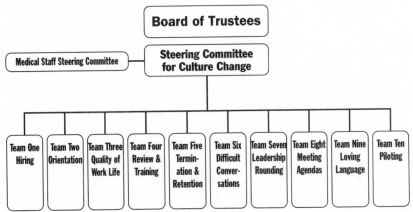

Board of Trustees

Medical Staff Steering Committee

Steering Committee for Culture Change

| Team One Hiring | Team Two Orientation | Team Three Quality of Work Life | Team Four Review & Training | Team Five Termination & Retention | Team Six Difficult Conversations | Team Seven Leadership Rounding | Team Eight Meeting Agendas | Team Nine Loving Language | Team Ten Piloting |

Here is a list of typical drivers of culture:
1. Hiring
2. Orientation
3. Quality of Work Life
4. Reviews and Training
5. Termination and Retention
6. Difficult Conversations: Counseling Others on Individual Improvement
7. Leadership Rounding
8. Meeting Agendas
9. Language (Loving Language)

A tenth team, a Piloting team, may be established for testing new work. The real process of growth doesn't begin with spring planting. It begins in winter. The farmers, the serious gardeners, the committed organizational leaders, assess their worlds. How fertile do I think my field will be this year? What is the potential in the organization before me? What tools do I have available? What is my strategy for growth?

Current Reality Check: The starting moment in organizational change is *where you are right now.* It's not a starting *point* because there are not points in time, only moments along a continuum which is far from linear. Peter Senge calls the starting place current reality. To determine your starting moment in living love, some key questions comes first.
- Are you ready for a new commitment to change?
- Do you know where you are right now?
- Do you have any idea of where you would like to be?

The question needs to be asked over and over: Are you ready to commit to living love in the workplace? If not, how will you live? Will you simply strive to sustain the status quo, hanging out in the gray half-light, living something less than your absolute best? Most people believe they have the potential to do better. This work is about that—about doing better, much better. The people you serve don't come to your organization because it's just okay. They come for the best. And they deserve it, don't they?

Throughout this work you will find us constantly mixing questions of individual performance with questions of performance by teams and organizations. That is because these three entities mix naturally in the workplace. My long-time colleague Tracy Wimberly likes to think of organizations from the three standpoints of organization, team, and individual. A current reality assessment will always start with an evaluation of all three.

ORGANIZATION

So how is your organization doing? Do a realistic assessment.

It's always interesting to me to see how leaders answer this question. Some start right away with financial performance. Since Sacred Work is directed primarily at not-for-profit organizations, I have always found this answer surprising. The real first question needs to be, "How well are you currently serving the people you were created to serve?" In a hospital, these people are patients. In other charities, the people are clients. Remember, nonprofit social service organizations were created to *serve,* not to make money. As a long-time CEO, I am well aware of the need for money. But with a nonprofit charity, money should never be the first question or the first answer.

Do the drill. Run through the metrics that you use to inform yourself how your organization is doing. Overall organizational performance is the province of senior leadership. How are you doing?

TEAM

The assessment of team performance answers a narrower question, but the question is no less complex. Team dynamics are critical to the success of the organization. There is no such thing as a successful organization made up of dysfunctional teams. According to virtually every indicator, the biggest determinant of job satisfaction is not pay or benefits but the employees' attitude toward their supervisor. If you're a supervisor, then, a big element of team performance rests in your hands.

Radical Loving Care does not support the concept of tyrannical leadership in caring organizations. Tyranny may seem appropriate for the chaos of a battlefield emergency, but it is inconsistent with the process of building a culture of Loving Care. As has been mentioned, this doesn't mean leaders are required to be soft and cuddly. There is a deep discipline involved.

It requires a real discipline to sustain Loving Care. How is your team doing? Does it contain members who are efficient when filling out forms but cold in their interactions with others? Just as important, does it contain members who are very kind and caring but never get the rest of their work

THE SEASON OF DOING

91

done? There's nothing loving about sloppy patient care. Members of each group described above need to be counseled using the Firelight Window tool on page 36. They need to be put on a six-month review path. At the end of this time, if there is not change, they, like weeds, need to be removed.

At the same time, team members who are living love need to be encouraged, nurtured, and rewarded in every possible way. Retention of great team members is even more crucial than the removal of weak performers. It is on the shoulders of stars that the foundation for a loving team is constructed.

How are you doing with your practice as a team leader or team member? What is your current reality? What's needed to elevate your team to a higher level?

INDIVIDUAL

Organizational performance can be seen as so complex that only sweeping gestures matter. The President of the United States or the Mayor of New York run such complex organizations that the best they may be able to do is create a broad vision and nudge the country or city a few degrees to the right or to the left.

But the individual is the complex building block upon which success rests. In some ways, this is the most complex category of all. How do you feel about your work? What is your current reality? Are you bringing all of yourself to work every day? Are you living your life around a set of transactions, or do you find you really care about your workplace and the people you live with each day or night?

If you are not bringing all of yourself to your work, then you may be working in the wrong job or in the wrong organization. It's more likely, though, that you need to find the courage to make a new commitment to the job you have. Like the man who has been married eight times, the problem isn't that he hasn't found the right woman yet. Instead, he needs to look in the mirror and ask some important questions about commitment.

The broad organizational effort to build a culture of love includes teams, but it really begins with the decision made by each individual, a decision made not just once, but many times each day. The Loving Care organization rests on each individual's decision to commit to live what we all believe in: to live a live of love.

STEP FIVE
TARGET TEAMS FOR CULTURAL CHANGE

Assuming the goal is to create a loving culture, how do you do that? The answer is for the Steering Committee for Culture Change to appoint a circle group, or team, to look at each driver that creates culture plus a Piloting team. Consult the list of culture drivers you created in Step Four. The Steering Committee should create culture change circles (teams) of five to fifteen staff members to look at each driver of culture, as well as a team that will be in charge of Piloting.

The chair of each team should be focused on its particular area in the context of change. For every group, the process is essentially the same.

Current Reality Check: Develop an *awareness* and *acceptance* of current reality in the particular area.
- What is the current process?
- How well is it working?

Vision Check: What is the vision for *integrating* this driver of culture?
- What are specific things necessary to generate change in this area?
- How would the process run differently if we integrated this change into the organization?

TEAM ONE: HIRING

Current Reality Check: Take a look at the state of the current hiring process.
- How is the process working?
- What are turnover levels?

93

THE SEASON OF DOING

- What questions are asked during hiring interviews?
- What are interviewers looking for in the interviewee?
- Have they been trained to watch for loving behaviors?
- Do they look to see if the interviewee appears to have a good balance of skills and compassion?

Vision Check: Good managers should know how to identify good potential employees. Remember that where attention goes, energy flows. If a manager is looking only for a limited range of capabilities, that's where the energy will go. On the other hand, if managers are actively encouraged to seek employees with positive attitudes and caring capabilities, that is what the organization will attract.

- Are staff, including managers, being recruited the way a winning sports team recruits good players, or are you responding to whoever happens to walk through the door?
- Are efforts being made to retain the stars in your organization?
- How could we make hiring more behavior-based?

In other words, in the interview process, every hiring supervisor must seek partner/employees who understand their work as more of a calling than a vocation. Any of us can be fooled, but effective HR departments and good supervisors will know and understand the right characteristics when they see them. *Hiring is the gateway to entry into the garden of Loving Care.*

Process: Use the Firelight Window on page 36. Design ways to hire the best flowers for your garden.

TEAM TWO: ORIENTATION

Now that you've hired well, how will you introduce new partner/employees into the organization?

Current Reality Check: Whether your organization is small or large, your orientation process needs to emphasize the IIF process. It should be **Inspirational, Informational, and Fun!**

- How is orientation running?
- Are new partners bored, or even falling asleep during orientation?

Vision Check: What would orientation look like if it was inspirational, informational, and fun? What are some things that might happen?

Process: What steps are necessary to ensure that fun things happen and

94

that presentations are inspirational as well as fun and informational? What if a small number of effective speakers presented all the information at orientation? What if game-style quizzes were used to keep interest up? What about prizes? What kind of music could be used?

Be sure you have, as members of this team, some people who are fun-loving and like parties. You need to have people who think in different ways about how to make orientation enjoyable. In large organizations, pick the three or four people who are the best presenters and have them do all of the presentations. A good presenter doesn't need to be an expert in personnel benefits in order to present the information. The expert can be available to answer tough questions, but the main presentation should be given by an entertaining speaker.

Some organizations are now using game-show formats to test new employee knowledge of new material. Why not? The goal is to inspire, entertain, and inform. This should be one of the easiest areas to change for the better.

Do lots of experimenting and get ideas from new employees themselves on how to improve. At the end of orientation, arrange to have each new partner/employee met by their supervisor. At Parrish Medical Center, each new employee is assigned a mentor. These mentors stay in contact with their mentorees for up to a year.

Imagine a new partner/employee's experience when the new orientation is put into place. Imagine a new staff member going home to his or her family that evening and saying, "Wow. My new job is already terrific!"

TEAM THREE: QUALITY OF WORK LIFE

It doesn't do any good to hire and orient well if a new employee leaves that experience, enters the actual work environment, and is disappointed. It's hard to overemphasize that the biggest determinant of employee satisfaction is the supervisor. A loving supervisor will have made sure the team is working well and the new member fits into it. The physical environment is important as well, and everything should be done to brighten it in a way that is consistent with the nature of the work.

Current Reality Check: Do new employees feel let down when they become a part of certain teams? What does the work environment feel like? What about lighting, windows, decoration? If the workplace happens to be in a basement, what has been done to energize the atmosphere?

Vision Check: How can loving supervisors be hired and trained? What

THE SEASON OF DOING

95

would the work setting look like if was significantly improved? At the beginning, don't think about whether or not something is possible. Just imagine a better setting. Make a picture of it. Now, how close can you come to creating such a setting?

At giant Riverside Methodist Hospital, Vice President Tracy Wimberly identified Quality of Work Life areas throughout the hospital. These included the establishment of a series of "pocket parks"—tiny areas outside where grass was planted and other greenery was improved. Inside, quiet spaces and seating areas were identified where employees could go to sit, rest, and meditate. Elevators were renamed using images like Apples for Elevator A and Cardinals for Elevator C. Intramural sports teams were established. The cafeteria was improved.

Process: Beginning with the parking lot and moving throughout the entire organization, look at the flow of partner/employee activity. What kinds of enhancements could be put in place that would improve the quality of your partners' experiences?

TEAM FOUR: REVIEW AND TRAINING

The annual review process for staff must recognize the concepts of Radical Loving Care. If employees are being reviewed purely on mechanical performance—time arrivals, number of absences, chart completion, compliance with rules—then mission is being undervalued. Don't worry about the fact that elements of mission work are difficult to quantify. The responsibility of supervisors in a loving-care environment is to use their best judgment.

Current Reality Check: Are staff members being evaluated based on loving behaviors? Are you using the tool of the Firelight Window to make your reviews meaningful? What about training? Is it effective? Teaching must always reach beyond mechanical task work. Change your training and teaching to emphasize that work in your organization is sacred and follows the teaching of Radical Loving Care. Make the review process an occasion to reinforce the vision of Loving Caregiving. What would the new forms look like, and what criteria would they include beyond what's there now?

The same IIF strategy used for orientation applies to training. It should be inspirational and fun as well as informational. Is it? What's needed to change that? Could the game concept be integrated into training so that training is more effective and less stressful?

Vision Check: In the ideal Loving Care environment, each staff member is being reviewed in a cooperative model by an A-level supervisor. If the supervisor is a C-type leader, it doesn't matter what forms you use—the review process will be a disaster. Every wrong behavior will be reinforced and the mission will seem to be a fraud.

Process: The tool of the Firelight Window allows you to establish three- or six-month pathways for improvement. Improvement processes need to operate in a cooperative dialogue. At the end of the review period, if there is no improvement, there are three choices: the approach needs to change, the employee needs to be reassigned, or the employee needs to be terminated. If there is positive change, pour on the praise. People are more likely to migrate to positive behaviors with positive reinforcement than they are with threats.

Effective trainers understand that pattern change requires trying out new behaviors. In Loving Care training, one of the most important tools is role-playing, and one of the hardest role plays is based on the prospect of engaging rude patients.

Role-Playing Training: Encounters with Rudeness

To learn how to interact effectively with patients who seem either rude to you or who may even seem "unlovable," envision an exchange and practice it with someone. But first, try to understand the dynamics that make interactions with certain people difficult.

Psychological Theory: When we perceive someone as a threat to us, certain reactions begin to fire into our consciousness. These reactions may arise from a primitive part of our brain. All of our training in cognitive thinking (which takes place in the prefrontal cortex) can be cancelled in seconds if we suddenly feel threatened. Psychologists have demonstrated clearly that many people engaged in arguments experience cognitive shutdown. They find it hard to engage in logical thinking. They may become meek and mute as lambs, or as dangerous as jackals. The animal metaphors are used intentionally here because reactions in stressful situations can cause some to adopt animal-like behavior.

How does the concept of Sacred Work help us in dealing with this problem?

Positive Mental Models: Instead of using negative thinking to block or cancel hostility, use positive thinking to create a better mental model. The best example of this I know comes from a friend of mine, Diana Gallaher, who described to me her experience of being confronted while she was engaged in a peaceful demonstration. "Suddenly, people were shouting at

97

me and blowing horns in my ears. Their faces were contorted with anger. They looked like mad beasts. But I stayed calm by repeating to myself over and over: 'This person in front of me is more than the angry mask they are wearing right now.'"

Professionalism: This can be a very mixed blessing. It can help temporarily, but it can also be the cause of the blank face on the clerk in front of you who may not be shouting back at an angry patient, but instead responds mechanical-voiced with lines like: "I'm sorry, ma'am, this is our policy." The best professionalism—the kind good doctors, counselors, and nurses display—is the kind a staff colleague of mine, Matt Deeb, saw at a clinic in rural Tennessee. An angry patient approached one of the caregivers. "He was big and scary and he was wearing a tattered tee-shirt and tattoos, and he was very angry. The caregiver calmed him down quickly with a single line: 'Gee, you must be having a real hard day today. What can I do to help you?'" Instead of meeting anger with anger, or anger with some mechanical line about policy or some authoritarian response like, "You're going to have to behave better," this caregiver simply engaged the power of her own compassion and humanity.

Martial Arts *vs.* Boxing: When I teach I often reference the Asian concept of martial arts as against the American idea of boxing. In boxing or, for that matter, football, the conventional approach is to confront force with force. In the martial arts, the core concept is to give with the opposing force and, in that way, to diffuse it. That's what the caregiver did in the example above—she let the negative energy of the patient move right on past her. And then she responded with love. I did the same thing time after time when angry patients would call my office during my tenure as a hospital CEO. At the very beginning of my career, trained as a trial lawyer, I made the mistake of arguing with people. I soon realized how ineffective this was. It didn't matter if I "won" the argument. There was no judge or jury around to rule in my favor. Instead, using loving-care practice and martial arts thinking, I learned to give with the negative energy. I routinely apologized for any concerns the person was having. This didn't mean I was confessing wrongdoing. Instead, my language was something like: "I'm so sorry you're upset. Hospitals are scary places. Let me see what I can do to help you." It was amazing to me how rapidly this cooled the fire of angry family members and patients themselves, not to mention upset doctors. Angry people are armed for battle. They attack and expect you to counterattack. When you yield immediately, they have nothing to attack but the air.

TARGET TEAMS FOR CULTURAL CHANGE

Love: Ultimately, our trainer is our belief in what Love and Sacred Work mean. Let Love be your inner trainer.

Here's a possible role-play.

> **Patient:** "I hit the call button sixteen minutes and thirty-eight seconds ago. Where have you been? I want to talk to your supervisor. I'm going to get you fired."

There are some very bad responses lots of staff may give in this encounter if they are not properly trained. One of the worst is: "Well, we just don't have enough staff here." This may be true, but it is not a truth that should be burden a patient. What is the patient supposed to do about the fact that the floor is short-staffed? Remember, the goal is not to win an argument with the patient. The goal is love.

> **Caregiver:** "You're right and I'm so sorry you had to wait. That must have been difficult. I wish I'd gotten here much sooner. I'm here now. What can I do for you?"

Nine times out of ten, this response will significantly diffuse a patient's anger. What about the tenth time? What about the patient who will simply not calm down? This is when it's time to look within yourself for courage. As Diana Gallaher teaches us, the person before us is more than the angry mask they're wearing now. Imagine this person as someone's brother, sister, mother, father, or child. Try to look past the anger in front of you to the frightened soul within. Anger is typically the product of fear. The patient doesn't hate you (even though they may be saying this to your face). Instead, they're scared. Your approach may not make the patient's anger go away. You can't always affect his or her feelings. But you can work to redirect your own feelings from negative hostility to positive caring.

Practice dealing with difficult people as often as you can. All of us have opportunities every day to do this—the glum clerk in the grocery store, the angry driver who cuts us off, the person who steps in front of us in the bank line. Every time something like this happens, see if you can ask Love what your best response might be. Above all, you are the one who can decide how you feel. Don't yield this power to others. Instead, consciously work to create mental models and patterns of thoughts that enable you to cope in healthy ways with the seemingly hostile forces around you.

Caregiving can be exhausting. Most people find it helpful to be able to ventilate to someone else the problems they're having with difficult patients, and talk about how they're feeling. Do this yourself if you think it will help. Find someone who will listen to you. And when a colleague comes to you, don't try to talk them out of their own anger. Ventilating means letting the other person blow off the steam that's been building inside them. If you try to tell them they shouldn't be angry, or they need to be more professional, you may come across as condescending, and you will also be cutting off your partner's ventilation process.

A hallmark of a loving organization, and of the highest form of Sacred Work, is the way in which staff handle not the easiest patients, but the hardest.

More Role-Playing

Depending on the size of your organization, the area of training can be a separate team. A role-playing team is terrific when the issue is dealing with problem clients or patients.

Current Reality Check: How are "problem patients" dealt with now? Do staff ever receive any training on how to deal with rude or unruly patients? What is it?

Vision Check: What are the *ideal* ways to deal with rude patients? Is anyone doing that now? Could those people help to teach others via role-playing exercises? What is the mindset necessary to deal with rude patients? How can that mindset be practiced and developed?

The following is drawn from a real-life case study of a leader dealing with a difficult patient situation.

You are a leader of a hospice residence. One of your patients, Walter, is a homeless, diabetic, double leg amputee. Walter shouts obscenities at your staff every day and night. His behavior is not only disruptive to the staff but to other patients. He likes to smoke. When he smokes in his room and a nurse gently reminds him of the no-smoking regulations he shrieks insults and obscenities. Some of the nurses want him discharged.

A previous supervisor routinely expelled such patients because she felt their disruptive behavior should not be tolerated.

Assume that the guiding vision of your hospice is to surround patients with love. But how is love best expressed toward Walter *and* your staff *and* other patients all at the same time?

A vision of love is fine. But what about the reality? What is a loving leader's best response?

Alive Hospice is an organization that actively practices Radical Loving

Care under the leadership of CEO Jan Jones and teaches it under the supervision of Karen York, V.P. of Mission and Human Resources and Debbie Baumgart, V.P of Patient Services. They use a multipart strategy to carry forward this love with *all* patients, including the hard-to-manage ones.

- Staff needs to know *all* patients need our love.
- All staff members need special training in caring for hard-to-manage behaviors because love can matter most when it's hardest to give. Love given to someone who seems unlovable is always a profound gift. Karen and Debbie both teach courses on Loving Care for all staff.
- Staff members need healing refreshment as well as training and support. Therefore, Debbie provides many opportunities for respite and renewal for her staff.

Debbie was confronted with a nurse who wanted to discharge a patient as difficult at the patient Walter described above. The following dialogue is the general idea, not a transcription.

Nurse: Mr. Jones is rude and disruptive, and I think we should discharge him.

Debbie: Our mission of Loving Care requires that we continue to care for him.

Nurse: But the previous boss would have discharged him.

Debbie: We have a new dedication here. We don't want to be just a good hospice, we want to be a great one. Great hospices don't discharge patients just because they're rude. They learn to practice love in the face of rudeness.

Nurse: Well then, what about practicing love toward me? This patient is being rude and hurting my feelings. Are you picking the patient over me?

Stop here for a moment and imagine what you would do. In the first part of the dialogue, Debbie has courageously advanced a new interpretation of mission, a new reality, to a nurse who has been working with an old picture of caregiving.

The Third Choice rule instructs us not to get stuck in a tyranny of only two choices. The nurse was trying to force Debbie to pick between her and the patient. Fortunately, Debbie did not allow herself to fall into this trap. She created a third choice, which appears in her response, as she replied, "This is not a matter of picking you *or* the patient. I choose to support you

101

both. This means that we will keep the patient at Alive Hospice *and,* since I believe your work is sacred, I will support you in any way I can in caring for this patient. I'm glad you're beginning Karen's course in Loving Care. Now let's talk about some other ways we can help you."

Debbie's response to this situation illustrates one of the ways Alive Hospice is moving from good to great. Most hospices have the same mission. Only the great ones practice mission by loving not only the dying, but the "unlovable" dying.

Whether a charity moves from being good to being outstanding is a moment-to-moment choice that lives in the hands and hearts of first line caregivers and in the decisions of their leaders.

TEAM FIVE: TERMINATION AND RETENTION

Leaders will sometimes ask me, "How can we practice Loving Care when we have to lay people off?"

Loving Care toward staff may count most of all when times are hard. During these times, love seems hardest to give.

Attorney and author Bill Banta, one of America's labor law experts, writes: "The major asset of any organization, regardless of the value of the equipment, is employees; it is your people—not your machines—who are the key to productivity and success."

In spite of the self-evident wisdom in Mr. Banta's statement, countless managers act as if this is not a true statement. The radiology technologist who told me once that he thought of himself as "mainly a button-pusher" suggests that he finds himself in an environment that tells him his machine is more important than he is.

A rich (by inheritance) and powerful boss of a major media empire told me once that "everybody's replaceable." He is absolutely mistaken. No one is replaceable. I hope that what he meant is that everybody's *job* can be replaced. But sloppy language of the kind he used makes one wonder if he thinks of his thousands of employees as interchangeable machine parts.

Achieving clarity on this point is critical in how leaders in loving cultures go about terminating and retaining staff. Although some people may say their biggest motivator is money, this should not be the case in charitable work. People don't choose social work, nursing, or counselor positions to get rich. They want to make a good living, but the best caregivers are motivated by a desire to make a positive difference in the lives of others.

The processes of termination and retention need to be handled with respect and special care. Always remember that the entire organization notices the kind of treatment given to terminated employees. People also attend to what is done to encourage and retain stars. Where attention goes, energy flows.

Current Reality Check: How are terminations handled? What is the difference between termination for cause and termination for elimination of positions?

Since laid-off individuals are not being terminated for poor performance or misdeeds, the use of security staff to escort them to their cars is inconsistent with the view of work as sacred, and it is disrespectful. Yet I have seen and heard of this fear-based behavior at numerous organizations. The damage to morale by a poorly handled termination or layoff is incalculable.

Vision Check: What is the ideal way for a supervisor to handle a termination? Could training be arranged to educate staff on how to do this work effectively? What are the key components of a loving message from leadership about a layoff?

Terminations and Layoff Discussions: Many of the same guidelines involved in counseling apply equally in the case of terminations and layoffs. Many people have told me it's impossible to practice Loving Care in the middle of a layoff. The reverse is true. Times of termination are times of loss. Loving care is even more important when someone is being fired than it is in the midst of day-to-day life. It certainly requires skills that may seem counterintuitive.

On the surface, terminations and layoffs are different. In the first case, the issue may be poor performance or may even be alleged malfeasance. In the second, the issue usually has little to do with performance. More likely, it's about money: there's not enough of it to support the position of the partner in front of you. But it's important to remember that even though an employee who is being laid off may have no real reason to feel personal shame or embarrassment, it is difficult to avoid these feelings, and it may be impossible to avoid feeling fear and uncertainty about the future.

As for terminations for cause, the challenge is to avoid treating such terminations as "occasions to pass judgment on bad people." As a former prosecuting attorney and judge, I am well aware of a judgmental tone that can slip into my own voice when I'm dealing with an employee who may, for example, have embezzled money.

When the work is sacred and the culture is guided by love, the intention is not to pass judgment. Freeing ourselves from judgmental thinking is essential to respectful terminations. If you are firing a partner for below-standard performance, the discussion should come as no surprise to the partner. In all but special cases, the groundwork should have been laid over several months through extended use of the Firelight Window. Here's a possible dialogue.

> **Leader:** In spite of our best efforts over the past several months, Bob, we're both having trouble making this work.
> **Partner:** But I've been trying really hard.
> **Leader:** I appreciate that very much. I feel as though your gifts might find better expression someplace else.
> **Partner:** I think you're making a big mistake.
> **Leader:** Maybe you're right. If you are, I'll have to live with that. Meanwhile, we want to offer you all the support we can during this transition.
> **Partner:** I want a list of specific reasons that I'm being terminated.
> **Leader:** We've spent the last several months discussing all of that. The hard truth is that this just isn't working. The better news is that there's a good chance you'll be a lot happier someplace else, and we going to help you as best we can while you make this change. Take a little time to think about this and call me. We need to make the change reasonably soon.

Don't expect terminated partners to thank you for letting them go or, for that matter, to like you. Terminations are heartbreaking experiences for people who have their hearts open. Since termination is a loss that can feel like death, the departing partner may even go through Kübler-Ross's stages of grief: denial, anger, bargaining, depression, and acceptance. They may never reach the stage of acceptance and may be permanently angry with you. That is one of the burdens of leadership.

Conversations concerning termination are as varied as the number of people that have them. The core principles of respectful dialogue are always the same. Show respect by being willing to take responsibility for hard decisions. Don't expect to be loved by someone you've let go. Practice Martin Luther King's guiding phrase: We must always be both tough-minded and tender-hearted at the same time.

When it comes to a layoff, if the cause is the usual one (saving money so as to save the organization), then you have a built-in basis for a respectful closing dialogue. Here is one pathway.

Leader: As you know, Kathy, we're experiencing terrible financial challenges. In spite of everybody's hard work, we haven't met our goals yet and the life of the organization is at risk. We've decided we need to lay off some staff (or eliminate some positions).

Partner: Does this mean me?

Leader: Yes. I'm so sorry. This must be very hard.

Partner: If you were sorry, you wouldn't be doing this.

Leader: What I'm sorry about is that we haven't been able to make enough money to support your job, because you are a capable person [if she's not, she should already have been let go or be on probation, in which case the conversation would be different].

Partner: Why me?

Leader: We went by seniority. [If you didn't use seniority, you have a more challenging explanation, which should be given with the same respect.]

Partner: This is so unfair.

Leader: I agree with you. Layoffs affect capable people, and it's a shame we aren't doing well enough financially.

Partner: Can't you cut someplace else?

Leader: We've cut every other place we feel we can.

Partner: I thought you believed in Loving Care and Sacred Work. This isn't very loving.

Leader: As you know, love requires be firm as well as being kind. We need to make tough-minded decisions to save this organization. At the same time, we care about you, Kathy, which is why it's so awful that we have to lay you off. I really wish we could keep you.

In a layoff, all of the explanations I offer above should be true. The hardest truth about a layoff is that capable people lose their jobs. You can honestly agree with and sympathize about the unfairness every person feels.

I have used both of the approaches described above. I have also been let go myself as, for example, when the company I helped run in Florida merged with a larger company. Senior officers may expect to be cut loose in a merger. Still, if you have truly committed yourself to your work and you are a caring person, it's hard to say goodbye to the people with whom you have been working. There may be less anger in a layoff, but that doesn't mean you won't grieve. In fact, every good counselor I know advises that it is healthy to experience grieving and not to suppress it. Find someone you trust who will share your grieving process and stay close as you go through it. If you are a leader, make this service available to people being terminated or laid off. This is the right thing to do not only for the person in front of you, but for *all* of your partners. Everyone is watching carefully to see if the organization is really treating the work and the people who do it as sacred.

Retention Reflections

Equal effort should be focused on *retaining* the best staff. Take a look at your organization's efforts to keep the best partner/employees.

Current Reality Check: What happens with employee recognition? Are awards only focused on length of service? What efforts are being made to retain stars?

Vision Check: What other kinds of recognition could be offered that would affirm the work of the staff? What extra steps could be taken by leadership to support and affirm stars in the organization?

An ongoing paradox of leadership is the need to simultaneously let people go while encouraging your stars and the rest of the organization with renewed energy. Here are two key rules for the times it is necessary to terminate one or more people.

Always let truth be your guide. Attempts to cover things up will always backfire. Fake explanations for departures, offered in the hope of "protecting" the feelings of the person let go, can be damaging fictions. Lies, even well-intentioned ones, generate mistrust.

At the same time, it is always wise to **celebrate the A-level caregivers.** This not only affirms those individuals but signals to the bigger B group the models of thought and behavior you hope they will emulate. Be careful not to fall into the kind of odious comparisons some parents make when they follow this process. We all know parents who have a star child and one who may not be performing as well, and the family refrain may be, "How come you're not performing like Susie?" The goal should not be a comparison of one partner to another, but a challenge to each person to be the best they can be using their own personal gifts. The behaviors affirmed in loving-care organizations should come from a balance of compassion and skill. Every member of the B group has the potential to improve this level of balance. The entire group needs regular reinforcement around this issue.

On many occasions I have picked up information that certain stars in organizations I led were considering leaving. Whenever this happened, I would never just write these people off. Instead, either directly or through others, I would actively engage an individual in a dialogue directed at learning the reasons for leaving to see if I could get the person to reconsider. This did not mean that I offered more money. It meant that I needed to: 1) signal to the individual how important she or he was to our success, and 2) get her or him to take some time to reflect on the change.

On many occasions, this two-part process got that star to reconsider and stay as a member of our team. And it was always worth the effort. Even if they left, they would sometimes return, discovering, frequently, that the grass wasn't as green in the other place as they had been led to believe.

TEAM SIX: DIFFICULT CONVERSATIONS— COUNSELING OTHERS ON INDIVIDUAL IMPROVEMENT

Difficult conversations with colleagues are no less hard in love-based cultures than they are in fear-based ones. But they have a completely different texture in an environment where work is seen as sacred. The fear-based leaders care nothing for the feelings of the person in front of them. Accordingly, whether the issue is behavior change or termination, the fear-based leader thinks of the employee as an object that either needs a mechanical adjustment or needs to be eliminated as efficiently as possible.

For those in love-based cultures, the hardest conversations have to do with staff critiques, terminations, or layoffs. The leaders of charities that understand their work as sacred are also people who appreciate the challenging and difficult nature of staff dialogue. How *does* a leader share with a partner the need for improvement?

The *Key Challenge* is how to promote a need for change in a way that nurtures positive energy and encourages hope. The *Key Problem* is usually an untrained leader who unintentionally lowers energy by poor communication.

Some solutions follow.

Mental Model. Rethink your mental picture of the person with whom you work. Are you tending to look **down** on the other person as a subordinate or can you look eye-to-eye as a partner? If you're thinking boss/subordinate, you become caught in a power model with you in charge and the other person feeling resentful.

Key Guiding Principles: Respect, Truth, and Uniqueness of the Person before You. How do you deliver hard messages without generating resentment? It's a mistake to begin by saying: "This is nothing personal." Anything interpreted as criticism has the risk of being taken personally. A second line that can be hard to deliver successfully is: "This is more painful for me than it is for you…" Although it is possible this may be true, it's a poor way to initiate a critique. Never presume to know another person's feelings. Never say, "I know exactly how you feel," because you *don't* and if you presume otherwise, you are insulting the unique nature of your colleague's thoughts and feelings. Instead:

- **Think Partnership.** If you and the person before you are partners, then you both share the same goals – the success of the organization or team in serving those in need.

- **Raise the agenda level.** "This meeting is about overall success and how we both can contribute to that."

- **Consider which approach is best for this person.** Some people prefer to receive information bluntly, directly "no frills." Others must be handled more gently. Try to know the person before you well enough to select the best approach for that individual. Your goal is to help awaken the potential of a partner. Find the best keys for that individual. Don't use a cookie cutter approach.

- **Check *awareness* and *acceptance*:** Find out the other person's current perception of the quality of their contribution. If you are concerned they are not reaching their targets effectively, first ask the larger issue of overall team performance: "How do you feel we're doing in attaining our team goals?" and then, "How do you feel about your own contribution?" You may find the individual is already aware of the issues and already accepts they are not doing as well as they should. If that is the case, then move to the integration stage.

- **Work with your partner in picturing what success looks like.** Help picture how she or he can reach it, and what support you can offer. Be clear about your expectations. Give your partner a chance to offer his or her critique about your leadership. "Am I supporting you in the way you need?" Make clear that you're holding them accountable for meaningful improvement. Encourage them in the areas where they are doing well.

- **It is time for the *action* stage.** Work with your partner in trying out the things discussed in the *integration* meeting. It is critical to go underneath behavior to motivation. If the individual is chronically late, why is this? Is there silent resistance, lack of ownership of the problem, or malaise brought on by personal issues? Is this person in the right role? Give the person a pilot period to try out not only new behaviors but new ways of thinking. Catch them doing something the right way and reward and affirm that behavior. What was the thought process underneath the positive behavior?

Larger Issues *vs.* Personalities. The Firelight Window enables you to aim the conversation at issues. This is about serving the mission and vision of the organization, not about personality. "I know we both agree that our patients need the best care possible. This means challenging ourselves to improve in every way we can. Do you agree?"

Role-Playing Difficult Conversations

Before diving directly into hard leader-to-partner discussions, consider how you would handle other difficult conversations in your life by first asking the question: How would *you* like to be given bad news? The second question is more complicated: Is the person before you someone who is like you or very different? Can you adapt your approach to the way *they* would want to be treated? Here is a possible interaction between a coach and parent and *one* way to handle it: the "larger issue" approach.

A coach knows he is going to have to tell a father that his son didn't make the high school swim team. The son has not yet been told. The father confronts the coach in his office.

Father: Coach, I know you've picked your team and I want to know if my son, Bobby, made it. He's got his heart set on this.

Coach: Okay, Jim, I'm glad to talk with you about that as soon as you answer one question first: What is your greatest hope for your son's life?

Father: Is this your way of saying he didn't make the team?

Coach: It's my way of trying to find out what your greatest hope is for your son, because Bobby is a fine young man.

Father: And a great swimmer as well, right?

Coach: Yes, he's a fine swimmer. What is your greatest hope for his life?

Father: That he be happy and successful, of course.

Coach: Right. Every good dad hopes that for his son, doesn't he?

Father: I guess.

Coach: I'm glad we agree, because I would love to have your help in working this through with you and your son on how best to handle the news that he didn't make the team.

Father: You've got to be kidding. My son is the best swimmer in the state.

Coach: You may be right, but I see him as a great person. As a swimmer, I see him as very good, not great.

Father: You're crazy. He's a great swimmer.

Coach: As I said, you may be right, but as swimming coach, I see it differently. I know you want to help him deal with this disappointment constructively. How do you think I should handle telling him he didn't make the team?

Father: That's your problem.

Coach: Okay. I can handle that. But you'll have a part to play when he comes home to you disappointed. What approach could you take that would help him deal with this successfully?

Father: Tell him the swim team is no big deal, I guess.

Coach: But it is a big deal to him at the moment, so that might not ring true.

Father: Are you trying to tell me how to raise my son?

Coach: I'm trying to help you with the goal you said at the beginning—that you want your son to have a happy and successful life. You and I have lived long enough to know that he's going to have unhappy things occur. The questions are, how will he deal with disappointment and how will you and I help him? Would you just think about?

Father: Okay, I'll think about it. But I still think you made a mistake.

Coach: I know you do, and if so it is my mistake, not yours and not Bobby's. I appreciate your coming to see me, Jim, because this will give you time to think over the best way to help your son through his disappointment and on to other areas of success. I know you want what's best for him. Good luck.

In this hypothetical discussion, note how the coach stays persistently on the larger issue and avoids criticizing either the boy or his parent. He also avoids saying things like, "This is nothing personal" or "I know exactly how you feel." In addition, the coach takes responsibility and even has the humility to admit, "Maybe you're right and I'm wrong, but I made my best call and I'll have to live with the consequences."

In designing this exchange, I tried to make the Dad fairly tough, but I know that parents can be even tougher than this. Fundamentally, however, the coach has set the key agenda for the meeting: it's about the son's *overall good,* and the question of whether he made the team, the bad news, becomes secondary.

In addition, he seeks to engage the dad as a partner in solving the hard news issue. Whether the dad agrees to help or not, the coach has taken the most constructive possible approach. Once the coach has done these things, he can feel satisfied he has demonstrated *respect* and done so *truthfully.* The hardest thing to recreate here is the third principle: the uniqueness of the person before you. I don't have room here to recreate the persona of the hypothetical Dad to adequately address this third point. But it is critical to know that your approach must be adapted to the personality of the one before you.

Work Application

You are a nursing director and you believe one of your staff is acting unprofessionally in the presence of patients. For example, she speaks openly about personal problems such as difficulties with her mother, trouble with her sick child, problems with her pets—and she does so in an agitated way that you believe may be unsettling to both patients and other staff. Otherwise, she is a highly capable and caring nurse. You want to help her correct the issue, but you are worried she's going to take any suggestion of problems too personally.

Your goal: to conduct a constructive discussion leading to behavior change that will make this nurse more effective and to have your counsel accepted positively.

Director: Thanks for coming to see me, Judy. I know you're very busy.
Nurse: Is there a problem? Did I do something wrong?
Director: I need your help and your thoughts in improving our overall team performance. Actually, I'm going to be asking lots of the team for their ideas on this.
Nurse: Sure. What do you want me to do?
Director: How do you think our team is doing?
Nurse: I think we have a good team. Although I wish Jane and Bob would work a little harder.
Director: What would you say are the top characteristics of a good team?

111

Nurse: Well, everybody pulling together to give the best patient care.

Director: That's a great answer. How would you describe ideal professional demeanor for a nurse?

Nurse: Neat and tidy, friendly with patients but still keeping a professional distance. And, of course, respect. I know that's important all over this organization.

Director: Again, those are great responses. I really appreciate your own capable delivery of care and how committed you are to patients and other staff.

Nurse: Thank you.

Director: As you know, one of the things that is also a big deal is that we keep our environment as stable for patients as possible. Since they're all so sick, we don't want to add to their troubles by loading ours on them.

Nurse: I agree. But nurses are human beings, too. We have our problems and I think it can help patients to know we have our troubles—it gives us common ground.

Director: That's true. It's also true that we don't want to overwhelm them with our difficulties.

Nurse: Am I doing that? I know my Mom has been so sick, and my son, and also my husband left me. It's been very hard for me.

Director: I'm so sorry for that. You are such a terrific nurse and I am grateful for how hard you're working in the face of your challenges. What I am hoping is that you'll talk with me about your concerns and maybe talk with our Employee Assistance Counselor as well. All of us feel off balance sometimes. I would be so grateful if you could share your personal problems mostly with me, the counselor, and your friends.

Nurse: Okay.

Director: Does this seem reasonable?

Nurse: I guess.

Director: Let's try this for awhile and see if it works. Remember, you're one of our best nurses, Judy. I hope we can work together so that you're even better. And I hope you'll help me improve as a leader as well.

Nurse: Thank you.

The key things to notice in these hypothetical is how principles are being applied. Conversations like the one above are often handled bluntly and clumsily. A director may say, "Look, Judy, you're talking too much about your personal life in front of patients and that's unprofessional. You need to stop that."

What's wrong with that approach? The best you'll get is a surface change in behavior. Since it was a unilateral order with no respectful engagement, the employee is likely to make mechanical changes in surface behavior. Meanwhile, he or she may well start seething with resentment over the abrupt treatment and may actively begin undercutting your leadership. If you're going to hurt them, they'll hurt you back.

It's hard to overemphasize the importance of customizing approaches to the situation. I've worked with people who might say to me something like, "Just give it to me straight. If there's a problem, I'll correct it. I don't want to go through a big counseling session." Maybe this is true. Tell such a person about the issue respectfully and give him or her the opportunity to make the desired change.

Genuine change is never just about behavior. It's also about affecting *the thinking* that causes the behavior.

Team Seven: Leadership Rounding

Rounding refers to any process the top leadership uses to visit the first line staff. Some CEOs make rounds as if they were admirals reviewing sailors. Figuratively, if not literally, they expect to be saluted by first line staff and mid-level managers under their "command." I have seen leaders conduct rounds in this way. It may be effective for the army or navy, or for a leader approach that is fear-based, but this approach is inconsistent with cultures of Loving Care. Work cannot be seen as sacred if the boss is the only important person in the organization and everybody else is a slave or medieval serf bowing down to her or him.

Leadership visits to the floors of the hospital need to raise positive energy, not create fear and distrust. Entire books have been written about the importance of this process, called "management by walking around" in the corporate world. Some leaders, like Dennis Swan, CEO of Sparrow Hospital in Lansing, Michigan; Jan Jones, CEO of Alive Hospice; and George Mikitarian, CEO of Parrish Medical Center, are extremely good at this. Others find it hard work and really need to be trained.

Current Reality Check: Do visits by leaders to the staff raise or lower energy? Why do some leaders seem to be killing energy on their rounds

113

while others are raising productivity by their very presence?

Vision Check: What if training programs were developed for leaders to be sure they are rounding to raise energy? What would rounding look like if it was done in ways that raise energy throughout the organization?

Leadership presence is, in many organizations, expressed most powerfully by *the way* leaders engage with others.

Magdalene Magic

If you pay a visit to Magdalene House in Nashville, Tennessee, you may have trouble picking out the leader of one of the most successful charities in the South. Becca Stevens not only dresses in a way indistinguishable from her staff and clients, but she is regularly seen working alongside them. She doesn't sit at the head of the table in meetings, she guides rather than runs the meetings, and she spends lots of time working to affirm the wisdom of others: "Great idea, Tonya! Good thinking, Maxine! What a good insight, Susan!" She is as likely to be self-deprecating about her own thoughts. Other staff tease her and she teases back. There is lots of laughter, lots of tears, lots of disorganized chatter.

How does Becca maintain a command presence in the midst of such chaos? She doesn't. Love-based leadership doesn't call for drill sergeant behavior or the need to occupy a fancy office or wear a designer suit. Nevertheless, Becca is as effective and firm and even fierce as anyone I've seen when it comes to advancing the goals of her organization and the troubled women she serves. In addition, I have seen her respectfully correct disrespectful behavior. If one of the women in the group is reading a magazine while someone else is pouring out her heart, Becca doesn't humiliate her. She says something like, "Joanne, your heart is important to us. Samantha needs your help and your best advice." She hasn't said, judgmentally, "Quit reading that magazine, that's disrespectful!" Instead, she has appealed to Joanne's better angels and called on her to share her best light with the group. As she does this, Becca is practicing love-based leadership.

People sometimes wonder how this approach can possibly be successful. It is, because Becca runs *the most successful* program caring for former prostitutes that we have encountered anywhere in the country.

Side-by-Side with the First Line Staff

There is no fixed boundary to human creative potential. You must become unshakably convinced that nothing is impossible . . . Make your own considered judgments independent of others' 'common sense' . . . *And in all your endeavors strive to position yourself in the center of the whirlpool.* [Emphasis added.]

—From *The Kyocera Philosophy,* Selected Speeches and Meditations of Inamori Kazuo

The idea of leaders working alongside first line staff is not new, but it is practiced far too rarely by CEOs caught up the idea of operating their organizations by remote control from their offices. I have enjoyed many fancy offices of my own—some of them a little too fancy. But the best work I did was never in those offices. It was out on the floors.

Inamori Kazuo, founder of the incredibly successful Kyocera (Kyoto Ceramics) and now president of the multibillion-dollar Inamori Foundation (awarders of the Nobel Class Kyoto Prize), may be one of the greatest business leaders in the history of Japan. He believes the key to his success has been his constant first line presence. David Halberstam writes in *The Next Century* (William Morrow and Company, New York, 1991):

> The high quality and the originality of Kyocera's technology resulted . . . because unlike the heads of competing American and West German companies, *he himself was always on the floor,* overseeing the kilns and varying the mixes.[Emphasis added.]

In fact, one of the best and most effective practices I ever engaged in as a CEO was the many hours I spent each month at Riverside Methodist Hospital working on the front lines with staff. Shortly after I became President in 1983, I got the idea to go beyond making brief visits to a given department. Since my goal was to signal to our six thousand partner/employees that the main job of leadership was to take care of the people who take care of people, I decided I needed to be out there working beside them.

But what, exactly, was I supposed to do? I wasn't trained as a nurse, a technologist, a food-service worker, or a housekeeper. What I decided I could do was to work *alongside* the staff, shadowing them, doing everything I could to be present while simultaneously staying out of the way.

The first key to making this practice successful was to block out four to eight hours on a given day each month to engage in this practice. How can a CEO do such a thing? A secret every top leader knows is that she or

THE SEASON OF DOING

he has more time available for such things than they want to admit. Sure, you can always stay busy in your office making phone calls, responding to email, reviewing spreadsheets, meeting with vice presidents. But where attention goes, energy flows. It's a matter of priorities. Every CEO can carve out the time for things that are important. I decided that time working with the real difference-makers in the organization—the first line staff—was important enough to take a percentage of my time each month.

The second key was to determine to make the practice *continuous*. In an organization, large or small, the appearance of the CEO in a housekeeping uniform will first be viewed as some kind of public relations trick. That's what some people thought when I began doing this work. The second month, when I returned to another department, put on a pair of scrubs, and spent four hours pushing a portable X-ray machine around with a fellow staff member, there was cautious optimism. A year later, when I was still engaged in this practice, people began to believe the truth—that I was sincere in my interest to demonstrate the value of first line work by exchanging my business suit and wingtips for the uniform of a food-service worker.

Of course some people teased me. "Can you empty my wastebasket, Erie?" a secretary might ask, chuckling at the apparent silliness of this request to "the boss." How do you answer? "Sure," I'd say. And I would smile, empty her wastebasket, and return it to her desk.

At first I was surprised at the fact that people seemed not to see me once I changed from business suit to uniform. It was a powerful reinforcement to me of the way so many first line staff may seem invisible. One day a surgeon was startled to recognize me mopping the floor with another partner in environmental services. "Hey, what are you doing in that silly uniform?" he called out to me. Concerned for the feelings of my partner, I excused myself, got on the elevator with the doctor, and said as respectfully as I could, "I realize this uniform may look silly to you, but the guy I'm working with wears this every day. And he's the one who helps keep this place clean."

"You're right," he said sheepishly. "Please apologize to him for me."

"I will," I said. "It might be helpful if you did the same next time you see him. Just thank him for helping keep the place clean."

The third key to this practice is that it *must* be grounded in sincerity. If you, as a leader, don't think you can engage in first line work with a real sense of respect and humility, don't do it. If you don't have the courage to take teasing from others about how you look in a dishwasher's uniform, stay in your business suit and focus on other things.

If you do this practice and keep your ears open, you are certain to learn valuable lessons and grow in leadership wisdom. When I became CEO of Baptist Hospital System in Nashville, I wanted to continue the practice. Unfortunately, I had to curtail this practice due in part to some health problems connected to a chronic illness (Crohn's disease) which I have lived with since I was nineteen. This held me back from doing first line work as frequently as I wanted. Nevertheless, I did give the practice a try on several occasions.

Even though this practice is highly successful, there are hazards to the ego of a CEO. One day I discovered I wasn't living with quite the humility I thought. On the first day I worked with him, Darren, one of our veteran dishwashers at Baptist Hospital, caught me up short. I was standing next to him, my hands elbow deep in very hot water thinking to myself what a prince of a guy I was to be giving up the comforts of my office to wash dishes. As my wife pointed out to me later, I wasn't even doing that at home.

"Darren," I said to my partner, "what do you like best about washing dishes?"

"Erie, I've been doing this for eleven years," Darren told me, glaring as he watched me place a dripping stainless steel pot on the wrong rack. "What I like best about this job is that I get to work alone."

He and I both laughed. But I realized he was holding up a mirror in which I saw that ugly edge of my own ego. I had been thinking how wonderful it was that I was in the dish room. Darren showed me I was mostly a bother to him because I hadn't yet learned his system and was slowing him down.

But in the broader scheme of things, the pluses far outweigh the minuses. If, as a leader, you stick with the side-by-side work and maintain a sense of genuine humility, the exercise will serve the mission *as well as anything you may do.*

Incidentally, by the next time I worked with Darren I had learned his system. And I told him I'd keep my mouth shut and he could pretend he was alone!

I never compelled my senior staff to engage in this practice. If they didn't feel it was their style, they needed to find another way to serve. At Riverside Methodist several leaders engaged in this approach personally. These included Mark Evans, Senior Vice President for Human Resources (who subsequently continued the practice into work he did as a senior leader at a newspaper and media company); Tracy Wimberly, Senior Vice President; Jeff Kaplan, Senior Vice President; Mike Greeley, Assistant Vice President; and the nursing leadership, under Patient Care Services Vice President Marian Hamm.

Many others did not. It is not the role of love-based leadership to force compliance. Instead, example, presence, and guidance are the keys. If a given senior leader didn't want to follow this practice at Riverside Methodist, their responsibility was to find other ways to express loving service.

I am convinced that the more than ten years I spent engaging in side-by-side work, from working in the laundry room to helping nurses at the bedside, was one of the contributors to sky-high partner morale at Riverside Methodist. By the early nineties, Riverside was mentioned in the best-selling book *Service Excellence,* by Ron Zemke, as one of the top three most employee-friendly hospitals in America (the other two were the Mayo Clinic and Boston's Beth Israel Hospital, led at the time by the legendary Dr. Mitch Rabkin). We were named in a national ABC News Special ("Revolution at Work") as one of the top ten employee-friendly workplaces in America. Similar honors were accorded to us by *Working Mother Magazine.*

Each person has his or her own rounding style. It is not necessary that every leader circulate as if they were running for congress. Regardless of personal style, the central elements of effective interactions with staff are: sincere interest, active affirmation, and meaningful followup. You don't have to be charismatic like Ronald Reagan or John Kennedy. You need to be yourself at your best. Examine your attitudes toward first line staff. If you are a leader, it's not enough to simply say, "Everybody is equal here." It will ring hollow if you are not sincerely interested in your partners. Each person has unique qualities that need affirmation and support from leaders.

TEAM EIGHT: MEETING AGENDAS

Everybody says they hate meetings. But organizations have them every day and night. Meeting agendas signal the values of the organization. Good meetings should be an effective mix of practical task work infused with spirit. You don't need to be a comedian, but it's helpful if there's one in the group. Light-heartedness energizes meetings and gives people the kind of oxygen they need to focus on the harder and heavier side of the work.

Current Reality Check: What happens in a typical meeting? Is the agenda entirely task-focused? If there is a devotional, is the sense of the devotional sustained throughout the meeting, or do you have the sense that the thinking is: Now that the devotional is over, let's get to the real business?

Vision Check: How can meeting agendas be brought into better balance? The culture of Sacred Work requires that Loving Care be woven through the subject matter of every meeting, not just in the devotional at the beginning of the meeting or through a speech from an outside consultant.

- What would meetings look like if they were seen as part of Sacred Work?
- How could agendas be redrafted to balance the efficiency of task work with continuing attention to ethics and caring?
- Do staff members feel free to raise questions of vision and values during discussion of business or quality issues?
- Do staff members challenge each other, including the CEO, respectfully but courageously in staff meetings?

TEAM NINE: LOVING LANGUAGE

In a letter to the editor of *The New York Times* (August 21, 2005), Barbara Tone spoke for many of us when she wrote:

> In March 2004, while in the hospital having a knee replacement, I asked a nurse when she thought I would go home. Without missing a beat, she replied, "Knees go home after four days."
>
> I remember feeling so hurt and angry. I had the instant image in my head that I was a knee, sitting in my wheelchair: not a person but a body part. It is a very painful memory.

Language is one of the key weapons used by tyrants to gain control. One of Hitler's keys to power was his ability to demonize/dehumanize any opponent, particularly, of course, the Jewish population as well as gypsies and political foes. It's difficult to convince people to kill other people. Killing becomes easier when the victim is referred to as "vermin." In this way of thinking, killing people is bad, but killing vermin is good. Once

Hitler was able to brainwash groups of concentration camp guards into thinking their job was to "clean out the vermin," his goal of killing Jews became easier.

Leaders who are not evil are susceptible to the same kind of ticks. If, as a boss, my *only* goal is efficiency and you are a clerk in the ER, then I might start referring to patients by number or by disease. Numbers have no emotions. Diseases have no feelings. Therefore, they can be sorted, kept waiting, or ordered around like cattle. After all, they're not *really* human beings.

If I'm a leader who's been required to make layoffs, I can keep my heart open and deal with each person with respect. But this is harder, more painful, and takes more skill and courage. On the other hand, if I think of employees about to be laid off as "units of expense," then I don't have to worry so much. After all, units of expense are mere numbers on a spreadsheet.

Current Reality Check: What kind of language is used to refer to patients and, for that matter, to other staff members?
- Are patients referred to as body parts?
- Are first line staff members referred to by leaders as "lower level people" or "the little people" or, worst of all, as "units of expense" or "bodies"?
- Do you hear the phrase from supervisors: "Have we got enough bodies here today?"
- Do staff address older people by their first names or as "Honey" or "Deary" instead of asking the patients how they would like to be addressed?

Vision Check: If work is sacred, then language will reflect Loving Care. Respectful language is important in the treatment of patients, clients, visitors, staff, anyone who interacts with the organization. Calling homeless people in the ER "frequent flyers," former prostitutes "hookers," and children with paralysis "cripples" objectifies these human beings. *Objectification is a key cause of inhumane care,* and its practice must be eliminated. Use the four-part Awareness-Acceptance-Integration-Actualization process to pull out these weeds in the garden of love.
- How can leaders set an example for change in this area?
- How could awareness be raised on the importance of language in a loving culture?
- What are examples of respectful ways to refer to staff and patients that could be developed and used?

As all of these questions are advanced in the organization, the culture drivers will change and the seeds of love will begin to grow and flourish. Some weeds will grow as well, and that is the reason for constant attention to these processes.

Healing Words, by Larry Dossey, M.D., is an excellent guide to the power of language as well as the power of prayer. I strongly recommend this book, especially for faith-based charities.

Other works I recommend highly are *The Heart Aroused* and *Crossing the Unknown Sea,* both by David Whyte. These books have been pivotal for me in understanding the power of language, including poetry, in appreciating charitable work as sacred.

TEAM TEN: PILOTING

A great way to test new work is to pilot it in one part of your organization. Take a given team and challenge its members with the opportunity to implement the phases of this work in their area.

One area where we tried this was the ER at Baptist where we decided to experiment with several ideas: 1) eliminating traveling nurses and other temporary staff and replacing them with more regular fulltime staff (to improve the stability of the culture) and 2) hiring with peer-group interviewing, an idea whose objective was to secure broader buy-in from the whole staff on who would join the team.

These pilots were successful and led to a broader effort in this key part of the hospital. Holly Kunz, R.N., the best ER Director I ever encountered, oversaw a complete overhaul of the 50,000-visit Baptist Hospital ER. By the time her team was done, patient satisfaction had shot into the 98th percentile, staff turnover was down sharply, and staff morale was higher than it had ever been.

Current Reality: Scan the teams in your organization. Pick one that is willing to pilot this work.

Vision Check: Have this team develop its own vision specific to its work. Run this team through the four-part Pattern Change Process (Tool #3, page 33). Ask the team leaders to report regularly to your Piloting Team and, when you're ready, to the Steering Committee.

THE SEASON OF DOING

PART FOUR

The Season of Being

Presence and the Sacred Encounter

Listening is an art that must be developed, not a technique that can be applied as a monkey wrench to nuts and bolts.
—Henri Nouwen, *Reaching Out:*
The Three Movements of the Spiritual Life

THE CAREGIVER WHO MADE A CHILD GROW

Several years ago, a story appeared in the British press about a young girl discovered wandering the streets of London. She appeared to be about nine years old. In fact, she was fourteen. Placed into the hands of loving caregivers, she gained weight and height at a rapid pace. One day, charts reflected that her growth stopped fairly suddenly.

Scientists carefully sifted through charts, records, food intake levels, and caregiving patterns to determine the cause. A couple of weeks after her growth had stopped, it abruptly resumed.

What had caused this phenomenon? The staff studied every piece of data available to them and finally discovered the cause of the girl's uneven growth pattern. It was an answer as simple, stunning, and elusive as common sense. The key variable in the patient's growth was the presence or absence of her favorite caregiver. This lovely nurse, with whom the child had bonded, had taken a two-week vacation. As soon as she left, the patient's growth tailed off. As soon as she returned, rapid growth resumed. Something about the *presence* of this nurse caused a dramatic and measurable change in her patient's *physical* dimensions.

Some will recognize *psychosocial dwarfism,* a condition that has been observed for centuries in children who have been severely isolated and abused. More recent is the discovery of the enormous impact of loving presence on the physical condition of these patients.

This dramatic case reinforces what all of us already know about the impact of other people's presence. In everyday life this phenomenon is more subtle. Yet it is critical to our comprehension of Sacred Work that we come to a common understanding about the enormous impact of our presence on the health and well-being of others.

A recent study, for example, suggests that male testosterone levels in many men will rise when another man walks into the room. Hormone levels in all of us may swing depending on the behavior and presence of those around us. This hormone swing often has a physical impact on our health and well-being. In another example, the well-documented White Coat Syndrome proves that heart and blood pressure levels in some patients go up the moment a doctor enters a patient's field of vision.

Since presence affects health, we need to become *aware* of the importance of our own impact on others and to *accept* the fact that this is something we can alter in a positive way. Presence is often signaled more by body language than by words. Body language includes, among other things:

- facial expression.
- tone of voice.
- eye contact.
- whether or not we seem to be in a hurry.
- whether or not we signal a sense of power over and/or judgment of the person before us.

THE RELATIONSHIP CIRCLE

Ultimately, though, the essence of our presence and its deepest effect upon others remains mysterious. Simple changes in expression, voice tone, and eye contact may improve our effectiveness as caregivers. But real change in presence must occur at the level of our intention. The caregiver who made the child grow did so not with her face, but with the power of her loving heart.

My younger sister, Martha, a receptionist sitting in the place of highest visibility in a large hospital, greets and serves hundreds of people each day. Most of them she doesn't know, but none of them are strangers to her. The moment they see her welcoming smile and feel her kindness, most of them warm to her presence. But to her, serving unfamiliar people is a calling. They are people in need, she is there to serve.

The Relationship Circle is a simplified model of how we may categorize and analyze our presence based on how we picture others.

Inside each of these categories are, of course, vast variations. Where do we see our enemies? Are they orbiting out at circle 5, as close as circle 2—or is the enemy in circle one where, as the old Pogo cartoon character said: "We have met the enemy and it is us."

It is also true that people within our own family may seem like strangers to us. Similarly, we may strike up a conversation with a stranger on a plane

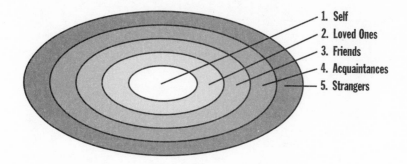

1. Self
2. Loved Ones
3. Friends
4. Acquaintances
5. Strangers

and, within forty-five minutes, feel like we've know them for a lifetime.

The goal of presence training in Sacred Work is to help us, in caregiving, to re-imagine those who come to us for help not as strangers, but as fellow beings in need. What if you took out all the dividing lines in the Relationship Circle and treated everyone equally? If stranger means someone not to be trusted, then we need to eliminate this barrier when the stranger needs our help. We need to build a bridge between ourselves and those in need by traveling with the mind and heart of the Samaritan, who reaches across the circles of uncertainty to heal.

ENCOUNTER
ANXIETY

Until a person confronts himself in the eyes and hearts of others, he is running.

—Father Anthony de Mello

People in need are already anxious when they come to us for help. And everyone who seeks the services of a charity (including a hospital) knows the "encounter anxiety" that accompanies the feelings of worry about whatever has caused one to seek help. We come to a shelter seeking food. Will we be rejected? Will we be treated with respect or condescension? Traumatized by rape, we enter a hospital emergency department. Will the clerk greet us with compassion or shove forms in front of us? Anxious about the results of a biopsy for possible cancer, we telephone the doctor's office. Will we be chastised for "bothering the doctor" or responded to with grace and compassion? Does the receptionist at the local hospice make eye contact with us?

The essence of Sacred Work occurs in sacred encounters, from the moment a person comes through the door. It cannot be overemphasized that these encounters take place whenever caregivers engage another's need with love. This may happen over hours or days as care is provided, or it may happen in a split second.

Sacred Encounters are not a function of time. Their success depends upon the quality of our loving presence. Caregivers who say they don't have the time to give loving care are not familiar with the meaning of sacred

127

presence. The practices described in this section can be very helpful in integrating a new way of thinking about presence and in putting this new thinking into action. The challenge is to explore our own ability to be present to the needs of others. This is not accomplished through mechanical acts of politeness. In fact, such politeness defeats true presence.

So how *do* we do this? The answer to this question is that the *doing* of presence arises out of our way of *being*. The good news is that if we are currently projecting an attitude of hurry and impatience, this can change. We need to take the courage to 1) become *aware* of the current reality of how we affect others, 2) *accept* that we can change how we think and act, and 3) *integrate* this change into new patterns of thought and *action*.

REUNITING WITH OUR SOULS: CAREGIVER TO SELF

The real voyage of discovery consists not in seeking new landscapes but in having new eyes.

—Marcel Proust

Sacred Work requires finding "new eyes." What we learn and think about others affects the way we look at them. As discussed in the segment about the importance of language in culture change, if I describe a person as a gall bladder, it affects the way I see both that person and myself. The person becomes a gall bladder. I become not a caregiver for that person but a gall bladder manager.

Awareness of language and the acceptance of the need for it to reflect love and respect changes our way of seeing. Sacred work requires sacred eyes, sacred hearing, sacred touch. Isn't it marvelous to know that you have within you the ability to find sacred ways of seeing and caring for others?

How do we see ourselves? Do we think of ourselves as children of Love or as cogs in the great machinery of a hospital or charity?

Our sense of presence arises from our ability to unite with our own souls. Our approach to work may have caused us to seal our souls in a lead-lined chamber. This begins to happen when our hearts are so injured by some insult that we withdraw. The insult may be the sudden death of a beloved patient, rejection by a supervisor, cruel treatment by co-workers, a

129

THE SEASON OF BEING

sense of drudgery or lack of affirmation by the repetitive nature of your work. It may also arise from a sense of rejection or disaffirmation in our personal life. The concept of Sacred Work calls us to nudge open the door to that chamber—to reunite with our soul. This takes work, courage, and patience. In the work environment, your soul may have been living behind thick inner walls for a long time!

Nobel Prize–winning poet Derek Wolcott describes this process of reuniting with our alienated self in his poem "Love After Love":

> *The time will come*
> *When, with elation,*
> *You will greet yourself arriving*
> *at your own door, in your own mirror,*
> *and each will smile at the other's welcome,*
>
> *and say, sit here. Eat.*
> *You will love again the stranger who was your self.*
> *Give wine. Give bread. Give back your heart*
> *to itself, to the stranger who has loved you*
>
> *all your life, whom you ignored*
> *for another, who knows you by heart.*
> *Take down the love letters from the bookshelf,*
>
> *the photographs, the desperate notes,*
> *peel your own image from the mirror.*
> *Sit. Feast on your life.*

How can we love others if we haven't developed a healthy love and respect for ourselves? How can we be present to others if we haven't first integrated our selves? We need to feast on our lives and, in so doing, reflect this joy to those around us, inviting them to join us in the feast of life. People in need are desperate to rejoin the feast table. Sit. Listen to them. Help them.

What kind of encounter is the caregiver having with him- or herself?

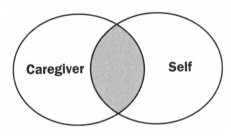

Much as I am trying to simplify all the concepts in this book and convert some of the practices to "tools," the fact remains that none of the practices I discuss are as simple and concrete to use as a monkey wrench. The Healer's tools are more like paintbrushes than they are like hammers and screwdrivers. The Healer's Presence is a prime example of this. Presence is not about adopting a plastic expression and forcing yourself to keep quiet as someone else talks. It is about respecting and valuing both the person before us and the situation we are in.

Partial presence in Sacred Work is problematic because Sacred Work requires full presence. The lack of it means I'm not bringing all of my gifts to bear to help the person in need. The problem is that we know that we're not present to every situation or to every person. Why? At a logical level, the obstacles to full presence may be boredom, fear, or the inability to understand *how* to be present.

1. Boredom: The person in front of me is rambling on about something I don't understand or am not interested in. Decision: It's too painful to be fully present. Instead, I'm going to daydream. We learned early in life how to look as if we're paying attention when we're not. It doesn't take very much energy to smile and nod while your thoughts are a thousand miles away. We can try Third Choice theory and try to change the subject, we can work at finding ways to pay attention. But the most popular choice is to bail out to daydreamland.

131

2. Fear: The thing happening in front of me (or to me) is so painful and horrifying that I cannot bear to listen and understand. In extreme cases such as child abuse, children may create, in cases that are famous but rare, other personalities. The genuine personality splits away because it is too excruciating to be present to brutality. In addition, children don't have the skills adults may possess to understand how to be present.

3. Inability: I'd like to be present to the person or problem in front of me, but I don't know how. For example, I am at a funeral for a child killed in an accident and I don't know what to say or how to act towards the child's mother. I engage as little as possible and disengage as quickly as possible.

SOME OTHER WAYS OF THINKING AND BEING

Since Sacred Work requires a sacred presence, we need to face up to the circumstances in which we are lacking full presence. A solution to boredom in repetitive work is to follow the example of people like Lois Powers, the cashier at Baptist who decided to tell jokes to people passing her in line. She re-imagined herself as a caregiver, not a cashier. Not only did she tell jokes, she was careful *not* to tell a joke to someone who appeared to be grieving. Instead, she offered the touch of her hand or a brief kind word. For Lois, her cash transactions in a hospital cafeteria became opportunities to give loving attention. It became easier for her to engage with her work because her work was both caregiving and fun.

A way to dissolve fear as an obstacle to presence is not to push it away but to replace it by moving your thoughts to the needs of the other person. As you think of their needs, your own fear is likely to dissolve. Another way to dissolve fear is to turn to gratitude. As you begin reciting to yourself that for which you are grateful, you will find that fear is running for the woods. Fear can't survive in the presence of gratitude.

The remainder of this section explains how to overcome other obstacles to being fully present.

THOREAU'S GENIUS TODAY AND THE DIFFERENT KINDS OF PRESENCE

We must learn to reawaken and keep ourselves awake, not by mechanical aids, but by an infinite expectation of the dawn...
—Henry David Thoreau

In his solitary retreat setting at Walden Pond in the mid 19th century, Thoreau explored the depths of his soul. His exploration took as much courage as one seeking to scale Mount Everest and it required even more insight. His report back to us, reaching across a century and a half, offers us a mirror for our own soul's journey. "I know of no more encouraging fact," he wrote, "than the unquestionable ability of man to elevate his life by a conscious endeavor."

The critical adjective here is "conscious." The routines of our lives can put us to sleep so that we are no longer present to our own lives. This phenomenon was demonstrated rather shockingly in the recent documentary "The Yes Men," in which a pair of pranksters traveled the world with fake credentials, pretending to be representatives of the World Trade Organization (WTO). In one scene, in a filmed presentation to an audience of businesspeople in Finland, one of the pranksters begins his speech with ordinary language and then sails into a completely ridiculous riff on the advantages of slavery and the values of monitoring your employees as if they *were* slaves. Nonsensical as the presentation is, the audience simply does not respond and, at the end, asks no questions. However, in a similar presentation to college students, the audience is outraged.

What's the difference? The college audience is still awake. The other audience of adults, caught in the entropy of corporate life, have become automatons.

"It is something to be able to paint a particular picture, or to carve a statue, and so to make a few objects beautiful," Thoreau writes, "but it is more glorious to carve and paint the very atmosphere and medium through which we look, which morally we can do." Awakening cultures from their dull lethargy and infusing in them whole new ways of looking is the exciting challenge of Sacred Work. Accept this challenge and you will find energy in your work place you may never have thought was there.

Thoreau offers us no less than a new calling to be present to our own lives. "To affect the quality of the day, that is the highest of arts. Every man is tasked to make his life, even in its details, worthy of the contemplation of his most elevated and critical world."

We know what sacred presence feels like because we have seen it in others, and we may have summoned it up from ourselves as well. By its very nature, presence arises from a still center, but when it bubbles to the top, it takes various colors depending upon the need of the person in front of us.

REV. DAVIS AND AUNT LUCY— CONTRASTING PRESENCES

Former hospital chaplain Rev. Bob Davis described to me sitting with a patient plagued with a severe migraine headache. He made sure the curtains were closed and offered the gift of his quiet presence by simply being there with the patient. "Suddenly," he told me, "the door burst open. In charged Aunt Lucy. 'What's up with all this darkness?' she shouted, throwing open the curtains. 'How is anybody supposed to get better in a gloomy room?'" The patient literally cried out in pain at this intrusion.

According to Rev. Davis, Aunt Lucy ignored this and began fluffing the patient's pillows and jostling his bed. Inside this small story you see the harsh contrast of two caregiving styles. Rev. Davis is in the midst of a sacred encounter. Aunt Lucy approaches with a different intention, one formed in her own mind *completely isolated* from any observation of what this particular patient might need. Rev. Davis is listening with sacred ears to the needs of the patient. Aunt Lucy is listening only to herself.

I am sorry to tell you that I have seen Aunt Lucy–type behavior from countless nurses who have the fixed idea that every patient must be addressed with loudly spoken plastic versions of "good cheer." Some patients may benefit from "happy" energy. Many will definitely suffer.

Many caregivers have lost the energy and courage to adapt their presence to the needs of the person in front of them. They have developed a rote way of addressing other human beings. This is like the tour guide we've all heard who is telling the story the same way every time. The boredom in his or her voice suggests a human being who has become a mere tape recorder that pushes the play button for each new group. We may hear that same bored voice from receptionists, from nurses repeating instructions to fulfill requirements rather than to truly teach, from leaders offering mechanical speeches to welcome new employees.

THE LOUD DIETICIAN

For individuals who think like Aunt Lucy, patients, clients, and other employees become objects, not people. This became evident to me years ago when I was shadowing a hospital dietary employee as she took orders from older patients. As she entered each room, she shouted, "Hello, I'm here to take your order!" Some patients didn't seem to mind, but several jumped at the sudden loud tone in her voice.

"Why do you speak so loudly to every patient?" I asked as we approached the ninth room.

"Well, some of them can't hear very well, so I've found it's easier just to shout at every one of them."

Easier for whom? I wondered to myself. And although I knew the answer was that it made it easier for the employee, I tried to suspend judgment. After all, maybe if I had to do this work every day and hadn't been trained very well, I might start acting the same way she did. It takes courage and energy to stay present to your work if it seems repetitive. But if every patient or client is starting to look the same to you, can't that be a sort of wakeup call? Seeing work as routine and boring can demean the self as well as the person served. This is what distinguishes people like Lois Powers, who sees herself not as a cafeteria cashier but as a caregiver.

THE SALAD LADY'S PRESENCE

This is also what distinguishes the work of a person I will refer to, here, as the Salad Lady, not to demean her with a label, but partly because I don't remember her name, and partly to fix the image of her in your mind for the special way she approached her work.

I was sitting next to her at a luncheon celebrating the work of employees with twenty-five or more years of service at Riverside Methodist Hospital.

"Where do you work?" I asked this gentle-looking woman.

"I work in salads," she said.

"How long have you worked in salads?" I asked.

"Every day of my twenty-five years here," she said with a smile. And then, perhaps sensing the question in my head, she continued, "You know, I love working in salads even more than I did when I started twenty-five years ago. It's a delight for me to arrange the lettuce on each plate with whatever else we're adding that day. This will probably sound silly to you, but I like to look out into the cafeteria every so often and watch people eating my salads. It gives me a good feeling."

"No," I said, "it doesn't sound silly at all. It sounds to me as though we are really lucky to have someone like you who cares so much about doing a good job. Thank you."

The Salad Lady found joy and presence in work which might seem like drudgery to some. She teaches us that each one of us can see any repetitive work we do as monotonous, or as a sacrament of loving expression.

SOME PRACTICES OF SACRED PRESENCE

Sacred encounters occur when caregivers develop a deep sensitivity to the real needs of others and an understanding of how their work touches others.

It is possible to take this to an extreme. I have known some caregivers to be paralyzed into inaction because they are either so finely tuned to the patient's feelings or, more likely, have gotten tangled up too much in their own. Some people who tell me they are "too sensitive" are usually stuck in their own roomful of mirrors, constantly monitoring each and every shift in their moods. I have heard people like this referred to as "so sensitive they're insensitive." These people will be ineffective as caregivers until they become aware of their overattention to their own egos and learn to work their way outside their house of mirrors and into the needs of others.

I am pleased to say that my own physician, Dr. Paul McNabb, has a fine understanding of presence. Each time I encounter him, whether as a patient or as a friend, I discover that he expresses the exquisite ability to listen well. He never seems to be in a hurry, but he is always efficient and effective. He studies the arts and is a model of physical fitness. In short, he exemplifies ideal presence in a physician. This is fortunate since he holds responsibility for training internal medicine residents from the University of Tennessee during their three years at Nashville's Baptist Hospital.

The key work in effective presence is always *balance*. The gyroscope that informs us about soulful equilibrium is located within each of us.

Here are some practices that can help us locate our best inner strength.

1. **Meditation and/or Prayer.** This practice is to be done in ways which are meaningful to you. Some practices may take up to an hour or more a day. Others take seconds. Some people view exercise

or yoga as ways to calm the self and reconnect with their souls. Still others, including me when I have my best days, like to take twenty minutes twice a day to sit in quiet meditation.

Many take no time at all. This is aa antidote for burnout and a certain way to distance yourself from life. Whatever practice you adopt, do something beyond what you are doing now, because Sacred Work requires deeper thought and reflection.

Holly Harris Smithey, a nurse at Baptist Hospital, once told me that she likes to say prayers at stoplights—a nice alternative to the anxiety lots of drivers experience as they wait impatiently for the light to change. Deadre Hall has been playing spiritual music in her car on the way to work for nearly thirty years. But she doesn't do this as a distraction, she does it as a spiritual practice. "I like to prepare myself each morning," she says. "I know I need to be a blessing to give a blessing."

2. **Power Pauses.** Kim Fielden Smith, R.N., former Chief Nursing Officer at Baptist Hospital, told me about a practice taught to some nurses in school. "One of the best practices in nursing is to teach staff to pause a moment before they enter each patient's room. It's a way to remind themselves that the patient they are about to see is special and is not the same person as the one they just saw. The patient doesn't just have a different diagnosis, he or she is a different *person* from the previous patient. Teach this approach to your caregivers. It is one of the things that will change the culture of caring in your organization for the better."

3. **Studying the Arts: Music, Poetry, Painting.** The story of seven-second viewing, told in the following section, signals a way in which art helps us to understand presence. The great contemporary poet Robert Bly said in an interview with Bill Moyers: "I wrote my poems by sitting down under a tree for two hours. This envelope around the body puts us in touch with the bark and the branches and the birds and the weeds. It's almost as if the tree said something in those poems. As if I heard that, *more than my own feelings.*" [Emphasis added.]

The challenge I offer is not that you need to try to become a great poet or painter or musician, but that you engage with the arts as a way of learning presence. Liz Wessel, a nurse with the Saint Joseph of Orange Health System in California, likes to craft beautiful creations called kabalas. Not only the image, but the process of making it, helps enrich her spiritual life, and this enables her to offer a special presence. Sit with a painting for awhile. Sit in nature. Let your lists of things-to-do fall away for awhile. Let your eyes see. Let your ears hear. Let your heart sing.

4. **Breathing.** In your spiritual practice to support presence, take time to do two things: 1) Listen to your breathing. 2) Practice *square breathing*—breath in for four seconds, hold it for four seconds, exhale for four seconds, rest for four seconds. Repeat this process for five minutes. Take care to breathe in through your nose and out through your mouth. You will find this to be remarkably restful.

5. **Eye Contact.** Notice whether you are making eye contact with others. This is easy for babies and hard for adults. Making eye contact is a powerful way of signaling to other people and to ourselves if we are truly in touch with the person in front of us.

6. **Mental Model Self-test.** Test the way you think of others by imagining someone you know and dislike. What is your mental model of this person? Why do you dislike them? Loving practice calls us to a higher plane of thinking and acting toward others. This means challenging yourself to think in a new and better way about this person. Can you do it? Yes. Will you do it? That's up to you. If you do it, will you feel better? Absolutely. Right now, that person is a negative presence in your life. But it is your image of that person that is sending drops of poison into the well of your life, not the person.

7. **Graceful Listening.** Since I have a version of Attention Deficit Disorder, this is often a difficult practice for me. For example, I suffer from flights of ideas which often come to me as I am talking with others. This causes me to want to write things down a lot, and my pockets are stuffed with endless notes. But I am aware of how distracting this practice is for others. Sometimes I apologize and ask permission to write a note, which is usually given. But such permission is no substitute for graceful listening on my part. Since this is a hard practice for me, I have worked very hard to let my note-tak-

ing obsession fall away so that I can be more fully present to the person in front of me. I've got a long way to go, but people tell me I'm improving.

You and I both know many people who are graceful listeners. What are the characteristics of their listening presence? How do they do it? Ask them. You may discover in their answer that part of it is a doing, but most of it is their way of being. Like magic theory, they may not know how they do it. They just do.

8. Apology. In light of our great fallibility as humans, we need to understand two practices at new levels. Since Loving Care is highly demanding, we are holding ourselves to elevated standards of relationship. As we climb these steps, we are bound to make some missteps. In the midst of fatigue, we may snap at our partners or at a patient. There are many ways to apologize. The most gracious is the Unqualified Apology. "I'm so sorry for snapping. I would never want to hurt your feelings."

But most of us give qualified apologies: "I'm sorry for snapping, but I was just trying to help you understand." Or, worse: "I'm sorry for snapping, but you can be so aggravating sometimes." In other words, I'm not really apologizing. I'm admitting I snapped and then taking back my apology or qualifying it in some other way. Qualified apologies are hard for recipients because they're hard to interpret. Practice the art of the unqualified apology.

9. Forgiveness. This is such a critical subject that it deserves an entire book. Here I reference it as a practice of Sacred Presence in order to provoke reflection. How are you doing at forgiving—first yourself—and then others? Forgiveness is one of the most critical practices of Sacred Presence. Freeing ourselves of passing judgment is difficult and yet important. If we have never practiced true forgiveness, then we have never know true love.

10. Oxygen and Breathing. Anyone who has traveled on an airplane with a small child or a fragile adult has heard the flight attendant's warning that goes something like this: "If the cabin loses air pressure, oxygen masks will drop down. If you are traveling with a small child or someone else who needs assistance, *put the oxygen mask on yourself first*, then on the person needing your help." There's not much we can do for others if we haven't cared for ourselves first. One way to care for yourself is to practice the relaxation technique called Square Breathing found on page 139.

The Season of Being

SEVEN-SECOND PRESENCE

Healing is the humble but also very demanding task of creating and offering a friendly empty space where strangers can reflect on their pain and suffering without fear, and find the confidence that makes them look for new ways right in the center of their confusion.

— Henri Nouwen

One of the most fascinating studies I ever came across was one that was done at the Chicago Art Institute in the 1970s. In an effort to understand the way average viewers engaged art, cameras were set up to record reactions. One part of the study measured the average amount of time a typical lay person spent in front of a painting: it was found to be seven seconds.

A parallel study was done with a group of art professors, artists, and art critics. The average time was similar—but only because the members of the professional group might spend an hour in front of a single painting and then barely glance at the next twenty paintings in a row. It was either deep engagement or no engagement.

Why does the average viewer spend so little time in front of masterpieces of art that took weeks, months, years to create? Part of the answer is that most viewers were engaged in purely *informational* looking. They worked with only a few questions: 1) What is it? 2) Do I instinctively like it? 3) How well did the artist recreate real life? In most cases, it took only seven seconds for the average viewer to get the answer to all three questions.

If the painting was entitled "Tree" and was by an abstract artist, most people were asking the literalist question: Where is the tree? When they couldn't easily get any sense of a tree, they simply walked on. Nineteenth-century viewers of Impressionist art initially dismissed Van Gogh, Cezanne, and other Impressionists because of the same limited thinking. Why didn't Van Gogh paint a sky that *looked* like a sky? Why did he use all those odd, exaggerated brush strokes? How crude.

Today, the average art museum visitor spends more time in front of Impressionist paintings than in front of any other group. Is it because they actually see more then nineteenth-century viewers saw or because they have been *told* they should be seeing more?

After hearing of this study, I forced myself to spend thirty minutes in front of a couple of different masterpieces. The experience changed my life and changed the way I think about presence in charity work. The first five minutes of viewing were fairly exhausting, leaving me wondering how I could look at this static image for another twenty-five. After all, I'm used to watching moving images, stories unfolding on a television or movie screen. I found myself wanting to move on to something else. "Okay, I get it," I was telling myself. "It's a painting by Renoir of people having lunch. It looks like people are having fun. The colors are nice. It looks like a summer day. What else am I *supposed* to see?"

Right around the fifteen-minute point, long after my informational questions were answered, I began to *experience* the work of art. Pretty soon I was having lunch with the group in the foreground. I discovered the astonishing still life on the table—a great painting in and of itself. Whenever love engages, I thought after looking at this painting, art is created—whether the art is a painter painting, or a caregiver caring. What an eye Renoir had, what passion, what commitment to lay down each brush-stroke minute after minute, hour after hour. But his genius went far beyond labor alone. Instead, his labor released *his* gift as light traveled through him.

Before my half-hour with Renoir was up, I also touched an edge of pain, almost in tears over the exquisite beauty contained in this single image—something I certainly hadn't experienced in the first seven seconds or the first few minutes. All beauty is painful, as is all love. Perhaps, I thought, that is why we are drawn to it and why we so often stop before we fully embrace it.

Through a copy that hangs on my office wall, I can revisit *Luncheon of the Boating Party* and find that I have a completely different experience. In fact, all great works of art benefit from our frequent re-engagement if our hearts and minds are fully engaged. If we are only doing informational

143

looking, it won't be worthwhile.

Those who have learned to experience great art as sacred know that we are different people every time we encounter a work of beauty. I have been listening to Rachmaninoff's Second Piano Concerto since I was a small boy. Since I was listening to it a great deal around the time I became ill with Crohn's disease at age nineteen, I lost the courage to listen to it for almost twenty years. Finally, at about age forty, feeling stronger again, I was able to re-engage with the thrilling surge of the opening notes of the first movement, the excruciating tension and release in its allegro phase, the satisfying strength in its coda.

The practice of sacred presence is a very difficult concept to teach in an instructional sense. The best any teacher can do is to create the environment for learning and encourage reflection and practice. Beauty, love, the sense of God, will appear before us only if we are courageous, persistent, and open. And if we are willing, as Parker Palmer urges, to approach as if we are engaging with the wild animal of our own souls. And how would we approach a wild animal? If we choose to approach, we will do so with a sense of awe, with care, with fascination, with anxiety, and with courage.

The experience of meaningful engagement of art will always help caregivers in their understanding of Sacred Work. In a half-hour conversation with a patient, what can you hear of their heart and soul if you are present to them the way I sought to be present to Renoir's masterpiece? Perhaps most astonishing of all is the degree to which an occasional half-hour of deep presence enables you to be more present to others even if you have only seven seconds with a patient.

It is the quality of presence that matters. The practice of deep presence over long periods helps us to rethink how we see every aspect of the world around us.

Sacred Work calls us to see the other person with a sense of awe, wonder, gratitude, and love. I think of a mentally challenged man I saw curled up on the floor at a charity called Outlook Nashville. I had some vague notion that he might be what I thought of as "catatonic." What if it was my responsibility to care for this man eight hours a day? How could I see my encounters with him as sacred?

I looked at his caregiver. Part of her was watchful as a mother making sure her two-year-old doesn't suffer harm. The rest of her was expressed in her eyes. She wore a beatific look of warmth, love, and compassion. Periodically she put her hand on the patient's back. It seemed to calm his groans. Her challenge was not that she had only seven seconds with her patient but that she had *all day* with him. In each moment she was gathering information to help guide her own caregiving, and she was working to keep her heart open so she could be present to a man who could neither speak nor respond to her sentences. If she followed seven-second presence, she might mentally check out of her caregiving role and, in her imagination, move out of the present into daydreaming. But that's not what I saw. Over the course of a lengthy visit, I saw her staying present.

It is immensely difficult to understand this kind of work unless you've done it yourself, which I have not. But on that day, I saw a caregiver and a patient engaged in an extended Sacred Encounter.

THE SEASON OF BEING

THE GIFT THAT'S NEEDED: THE SACRED AND THE PROFANE

The late Rev. Bob Davis, Vice President for Pastoral Care at Riverside Methodist Hospital, once advised me that loving care offers the gift that is needed. It may be a few thoughtful words, it may be silent presence, it may be the gift of unconditional love to someone who doesn't seem to even know you're there.

Many leaders and caregivers who are more extroverted may have difficulty learning the power of silent presence. My dad, a wonderful leader for fifty years with the YMCA, raised me to believe that it was my responsibility as a leader to carry conversations, to fill in empty spaces with my own thoughts. This was sometimes a handy skill if I was, for example, hosting a television and radio health show as I did for eight years in Columbus, or if I was suddenly called on to give an improvisational speech. It also helped me during my seven years as a trial lawyer.

But it's often not a useful skill in more intimate personal conversation. There you have the opportunity to watch and listen for what the other person needs. Caregiving often involves one-on-one attention to people in pain. What is the gift they need from us beyond technical skill? Bev Smith, a leader at Riverside Methodist, told the following powerful story about an experience she had during her time as an administrative fellow in 1992:

> On one particular evening, I walked by a patient's room in the Critical Care Unit and noticed a woman lying very still as tubes flowed into her and a monitor beeped a faint but steady reminder to "hold on." I noted "Lewis" written on the name card near the door. Although the woman didn't seem

146

to hear, I chatted with her for a moment, something about the weather, I think, then quietly left the room with a wave of goodbye. For fifteen straight nights I stopped by Ms. Lewis's room to say hello for a moment. Ms. Lewis never moved or opened her eyes in response.

On the sixteenth evening, I was in a bit of a hurry, so I waved a quick "Hello, Ms. Lewis" as I sped past the door, only to hear a faint "Hello" drift from the room. I rapidly retraced my steps, walked into Ms. Lewis's room, and looked down into a smiling pair of blue eyes. Ms. Lewis reached for my hand and said in a whisper, "I waited for you. Every evening I waited for you to stop in my room and talk to me. It made the nights bearable. Thank you, young lady."

This kind of loving care can be just as important when given from partner to partner. My younger sister Martha, a receptionist at The Toledo Hospital, a seven hundred–bed medical center with thousands of employees, told me a story that demonstrates the impact of split-second encounters. Each morning as she makes her way from the parking lot to the front door, Martha likes to say "Good Morning" to the night shift staff that, coming off work, pass her in the opposite direction. "Most people smile and respond," she told me. "About a year ago, I noticed that one nurse never did. She would just walk by me morning after morning as if I hadn't said a thing. But I made a point of saying hello to her anyway. Toward the end of the year, I saw this nurse coming toward me. I said hello as always. Suddenly she handed me a note and walked on. The note said: 'Thank you for always giving me such a cheery greeting every morning. You always brightened my day and made me feel like I mattered. I never answered you because I am just so terribly shy. Thank you for your kindness.'"

Most of the time we never know the impact of the loving acts we do. It was wonderful for Martha to receive this note. But she would have continued saying hello whether or not her kindness was ever acknowledged.

Countless caregivers deliver acts of lovingkindness every day and night toward people who have no ability to express thanks. This is the regular work of support-givers at places like Outlook Nashville where first line staff care for profoundly mentally challenged adults and medically fragile children. I see it at the Park Center where staff cares for individuals with significant mental illness and at a section of McKendree Village where partners care for patients with dementia. It happens every day and night in America's operating and recovery rooms and intensive care nurseries where staff look after patients who lack the ability to express appreciation.

These are settings where loving care can shine, as well as in those places where, in the presence of bad leadership, patients can be abused, neglected, and/or ignored. It takes enormous energy and commitment to deliver care to those in altered states of consciousness. There is always the risk of falling into a disastrous thought pattern that delivers the message, "Who cares? This person in front of me can't tell whether I'm being nice or not. Why make the effort?"

Sad to say, some staff think of their work not as sacred, but as mechanical—as if they were employed in meat freezers or were herding cattle. Unconscious surgical patients become "sides of beef," the mentally challenged are seen as "retards," and crying babies can become "squealers."

Remember the role of language and how this impacts thought. Everyone working in tough areas like those described above may fall into an occasional joking line. But regular patterns of talk and the labels used will reflect whether the thought process is loving and respectful or demeaning and denigrating.

The surprise, here, is that when first line staff fall into the negative line of thinking, they instantly demean not only their work but themselves. They have reduced their work to being custodians of unconscious people and reduced themselves to mean-spirited beings. Their work becomes not sacred, but profane.

ENGAGING THE HEARTS OF STAFF IN SACRED WORK

L eaders should never assume full acceptance of a new vision and practice simply because staff are nodding their heads. In many organizations, even enlightened ones, staff members are trained to nod in agreement to anything an appointed leader suggests. Even though there may appear to be acceptance, this does not mean any given partner has *integrated* a new pattern of thought into his or her mental models.

STAFF MEMBER WISDOM AND ART

A critical way to develop and enrich staff thinking is to challenge each person to take a try at writing their own ways of describing wisdom and love. The results will be beautiful, as reflected in the words below, composed between 1991 and 1993 by members of the leadership team at Riverside Methodist Hospital. I have added a comment (number 10) made to me by a housekeeper on staff at Baptist Hospital, whom I interrupted one day with the question: "How would you describe loving care?" This is the kind of beauty and wisdom that pours out when you urge staff members to share their own insights and feelings in writing.

See if you can identify the job description of each of the following writers.

    1. *We need, in caregiving, the strength and the wisdom and the skill to walk beside those who need our help so that they may leave here cured and healed.*

                —Jim Wesley, Vice President for Information Systems

2. *Hope is a powerful medicine,*
   Sometimes it alone makes pain bearable . . .
   It helps you give the gift itself to those for whom you care.
   —Frank Pandora, Esq., Senior Vice President
   and Legal Counsel

3. *We seek the wisdom, patience, and understanding to do the right*
   thing, to look beyond short-term reward for long-term improvement
   in human caring.
   —Nancy Schlichting, Chief Operating Officer

4. *We express caring when we guide a lost visitor to the right room, when*
   we take a moment to pick up the errant candy wrapper, when we spend
   the extra moment to explain a complicated procedure to a patient and
   their family members, or when we simply stop by a lonely patient's room
   to chat a moment about the weather.
   —Bev Smith, Administrative Intern

5. *Help keep our hearts and minds focused on the good we can do for one*
   another—together.
   —Mike Greeley, Assistant Vice President.

6. *Help us to be kind and caring and loving with our family, friends, col-*
   leagues, and those we've yet to meet.
   —Debbie Phillips, Director of Public Relations

7. *Help us to always be mindful of the opportunity we have to foster an*
   environment of positive, supportive, covenantal relationships.
   —Mark Evans, Sr. Vice President, Human Resources

8. *Help us search for your love through our differences . . .*
           —Jim Wheaton, Vice President, Planning

9. *We all hurt for different reasons/We all need strength/To make ourselves whole and/To make the world around us whole.*
           —Mark Feinknoph, Hospital Architect

10. *Loving care means helping other people no matter what.*

CHERISHING CAREGIVERS IN GOLDEN HOURS

The word *cherish* is used in wedding ceremonies, but I rarely hear it spoken elsewhere. To cherish—it's a beautiful verb phrase. Gandhi demonstrated that he cherished the work of fellow Indians by working alongside them. Mother Teresa demonstrated that she cherished the poorest of the poor in Calcutta by literally touching people labeled "untouchable." One way Jesus demonstrated how much he cherished his disciples was by washing their feet. In Nashville, the Magdalene charity carries this practice forward with a ceremony in which all staff wash each other's feet.

Labeling a group of people "untouchable" is, by the way, a powerful way to demonstrate the importance we attach to being touched. Saying someone is such a pariah they are not to be touched is a terrible punishment, akin to shunning someone from society. To cut someone off from communication, touching, human contact, to put them into solitary confinement and to exile them from the community, is thought to be one of the harshest punishments we can give. Babies not touched will lose weight and often die no matter how much food they are given. Shunned human beings experience suppressed immune systems and become more vulnerable to illness.

Conversely, how does a community make its members feel welcome and honored? Imagine if you, as a caregiver at a nursing home, a crisis worker at a teen center, or a nurse on a hospital floor, felt cherished as a partner of the organization. Wouldn't you feel even more likely to express loving care to those around you? Would you also feel more productive, more dedicated to the organization's mission, less inclined to leave?

Since all of these outcomes are what leaders seek, how can leaders express to their first line partners this beautiful notion of cherishing? This is the challenge this work poses to every leader. If these words have turned your attention to cherishing, you are becoming *aware*. If you accept that this is something your organization should tackle, what can you do to help your partners feel cherished?

The caregiving practices described in this book include some suggestions which are *not* comprehensive. It's a good idea to create a Culture Circle for each practice to brainstorm pictures of leader behaviors that can advance the practice. This is how *integration* is practiced: picture new behaviors—how would each area look if things were done in a more loving way?

There is real genius inside the thinking and the practice of each of the following ideas. They reinforce the importance of democratic leadership, and they signal why it is that high-control leaders hate the whole notion of work as sacred. Loving cultures are fertile ground for creative thinking, high energy, and high productivity. Partner/employees thrive in the presence of guidelines that provide general boundaries rather than rules that constrict effective work. This is one more reason that organizations that engage the power of Sacred Work thrive while other organizations wither in the desert of the status quo or the caves of fear.

Caring Blitzes

It's a strange-sounding phrase. You may want to pick another way to describe it. But I hope this phrase grabs your attention. Here is what's involved: Good leaders make rounds in their organization on a regular basis. If it's a hospital, they walk the organization floor by floor and unit by unit like honeybees spreading their healing through presence. If the organization is smaller, leaders make it a point to round by engaging their staff whenever possible to offer support and affirmation. This is still known in some circles as "management by walking around."

Rounding is one of the most significant ways leaders affirm and advance the mission and vision of the organization. The challenge is that some leaders are stunningly ineffective at this. I have seen first line staff people literally wince in pain as they see certain leaders approaching their areas. "Oh no, here he/she comes!" they seem to be saying. Leaders who round like this are often the old clipboard types who patrol the areas of their responsibility like guards checking prison cells. Their goal is not to help encourage and support staff. They may use rounding as one of their tools of intimidation, to demonstrate who is boss and to spread fear.

Leaders in a loving organization should gather periodically to share ideas on the best ways to show the staff they are valued. The characteristics of good rounding are a demonstration of exactly the kinds of behaviors leaders are trying to reinforce. If the goal is to create caring, leaders must show caring by: a) good listening, b) rapid follow-through on legitimate issues, c) real interest in the lives of staff, d) warmth and affirmation.

Caring blitzes are a step beyond good rounding. They include more of the above and a little extra beyond that. Blitzes require more time than typical rounding and would ordinarily be done no more often than once a month. They may be occasions when leaders go to the floor as a group to further honor a twenty-five-year partner or a new mom or a partner who has won a compassion award. In a large organization, a single department might be "blitzed." Blitzes can include material things like free pizza coupons or game tickets, but the real goal is to signal a deeper kind of caring.

At the more poignant end of the spectrum, these rounds can be occasions when leaders signal sympathy for partners who have experienced loss. Beyond personal sympathy, I often tried to send notes to employees who experienced any kind of personal difficulty including divorce and illness as well as a death in the family. In real caring organizations, leaders take the time to attend the weddings and funerals of staff.

These thoughts represent a few suggestions, but the real effectiveness has to do with *how* leaders communicate presence. Cherishing is a beautiful thing when it's sincere and ugly and silly when it's faked. The only way to express cherishing is for leaders first to look into their own hearts and develop and nurture real feelings for the staff with whom they work.

The lovely Sonoma Valley north of San Francisco experiences many hours of golden sunlight. But there are golden hours of light inside Santa Rosa Hospital (part of the Saint Joseph of Orange Health System) as well. Two hours twice a week are reserved by leadership as Golden Hours. During these two hours on two different days of the week (one morning and one evening), leaders are not allowed to schedule anything on their calendars. Instead, they are expected to be up on the floors visiting first line staff, raising spirits, learning what's on the hearts and minds of the various teams, and spreading the message of vision through presence. Under the leadership of President George Perez, these rounds are viewed as a key element of success in building the morale of first line staff. George, in particular, makes it a point to spend significant blocks of time on the floors. He understands the power of leading by presence, and patient and employee satisfaction are both improved as a result.

Partner Recognition

Every organization has employee recognition events. But do these events really give employees a sense of being cherished? Often employee recognition means nothing more than issuing pins to staff for years of service. Employees file through lines past bored managers who hand them their awards as if they are issuing hall passes. What could you, as a leader, do to enrich this event, to make it an occasion through which partners felt *deeply* honored?

At 1000-bed Riverside Methodist Hospital in the 1980s and early '90s, I challenged the staff to deepen the meaning of this event. The results were astounding. Under the leadership of Senior H.R. Vice President Mark Evans, the event became one of the finest recognition events in the country. We created an event that went on for months, not just one day. Special occasions were designed to honor ten- and fifteen- and twenty-year employees as separate groups, new awards were designed to recognize caring and compassion (where attention goes, energy flows), and senior leaders attended all of these sessions not out of obligation but because it is a joy to honor staff. These pre-events culminated in a lovely extravaganza in which name performers were hired to entertain the staff at a evening gala at a downtown Columbus theater.

Whatever you choose to do, couldn't a culture circle help you improve the quality of your recognition event?

Treatment for Compassion Fatigue

As mentioned in Step One of Part Three, one way leaders demonstrate cherishing is by recognizing that caregivers experience exhaustion in their work. One phrase for this is *compassion fatigue*. Caring Circles made up of staff that meet once a week or once a month can provide an opportunity for healing by giving each partner in a circle a few minutes to express their frustration and fatigue and to listen to the difficulties and joys of others.

Mentoring

One of the best examples of a good mentoring program was put in place by George Mikitarian's team at Parrish Medical Center. During and after orientation, each new employee is assigned a mentor, a veteran employee who has agreed to work in the mentoring program and act as a partner to newcomers. Imagine the power of this idea!

- Orientation now continues for weeks and months afterwards through the light of this mentor.
- The mentor becomes a teacher and hears himself or herself reinforcing all the best values of the organization each moment they mentor.
- The new employee receives the gift of one-on-one attention from a veteran specifically assigned to make his or her new experience as good as possible.

Foot-Washing and The Moccasin Exercise

We've all heard the phrase, derived from Native American wisdom, about not judging another person until you've "walked in his moccasins for a long time."

There are at least two ways to do this. One is to rotate people around in their jobs for brief periods. At the Campus for Human Development, an organization which deals with the homeless, everyone takes a turn at staffing the check-in desk. The same should be done more often at hospitals. Job exchange is a great way to breed understanding and to improve communication.

A less common but also effective approach is for leaders to work in first line roles as much as possible. This is not a strict exchange because the first line person would not, in this example, take over the leader's role (although that can sometimes be a helpful exercise as well). What is suggested here, for those with the energy and sincerity to do it, is that leaders literally work shifts in first line jobs. The larger the organization, the more helpful this can be. See pages 114–118 for more information on this practice, and my own experiences with it.

There is a tendency, particularly among many nursing leaders, to doff their scrubs in favor of fancy suits when they get promoted. This is an unfortunate trend and can, unconsciously, cause leaders to begin to distance themselves from their first line caregivers. I understand the need for business clothes. But making changes every so often can send a great signal to your teams.

One of history's finest examples of the practice of humility is the story of Jesus washing the feet of his disciples. Magdalene founder Rev. Becca Stevens, in her marvelous book *Finding Balance,* describes this story in a way that is beautifully applicable to her work with former prostitutes. As mentioned above, the organization regularly models Jesus' foot-washing example by performing ritual foot-washing with each other using the soothing products produced by the organization's subsidiary, Thistle Farms.

It is the challenge of the leader to ensure that *no* one ever feels "lowly" in the organization. The way to do this is to continually christen everyone as caregivers and to demonstrate over and over every day that the key work of the organization is done through the hearts and hard work of the first line teams.

RENEWAL AND THE
GOLDEN THREAD

Try? There is not try. There is only do, or not do.

—Yoda

Imagine that you planted a garden and nurtured it to success by watering and fertilizing and weeding and replanting and spraying and tending, and you did this each year for a dozen years. Now, can you imagine that the garden would grow just as well if you ignored it?

The idea that the garden of loving care needs constant nourishing cannot be overemphasized. It is true that once the culture has been established, many aspects of it become easier. A good culture, just like a bad one, begins to reinforce itself through the actions of staff members who live its patterns.

But the wrong leader can kill a loving culture with the embrace of cold and controlling hands. I have seen the wrong leaders chill the warmth of Radical Loving Care with arrogance and power games. Ultimately, it is the responsibility of the board of trust to exert a guiding hand over a misdirected leader. But boards are often kept at a distance by high-control CEOs.

It takes enormous commitment to create the right culture. As with so many examples of living beauty, a single storm can destroy it. Board members need to tend the garden. They need to be sure the right gardener is engaged in the right practices or lots of fine and loving work will be extinguished.

First line staff can play a role as well. They need to stand strong against any leader who threatens the essential commitment of Sacred Work. History reflects that most things move in cycles and everything is dynamic. At the same time, certain cultures have been able to sustain themselves at high-quality levels for centuries. American universities like Harvard and Yale and certain European universities like Oxford, Cambridge, the Sorbonne, and the great universities of Italy have developed and sustained traditions of excellence for generation upon generation. The Mayo Clinic is building a tradition of caring and excellence that is so strong it is likely to endure for hundreds of years.

Despite many perversions and wrong twists in the behavior of some of their leaders along the way, the essential tenets of the Jewish, Christian, Muslim, Hindu, and Buddhist faiths remain intact. They are evidence that essential truth can endure in the institutions of civilization.

These examples give hope that the Golden Thread of loving care can be deeply woven into the fabric of an organization. Love is the highest and most noble expression of the human condition. Its torch rests in the hands of today's caregivers who have the choice to let it fall to the ground or to hold it high so it may warm and illuminate the lives of all who need it.

In his provocative book *Mere Christianity*, the great C.S. Lewis wrote:

> Do not waste your time bothering whether you "love" your neighbor, act as if you did. As soon as we do this, we find one of the great secrets. When you are behaving as if you loved someone, you will presently come to love him. If you injure someone you dislike, you will find yourself disliking him more. If you do him a good turn, you will find yourself disliking him less.

Lewis tries to help us make love easier, to say that after all, there is something in it for us, that if you love your neighbor even if you don't *like* him or her, you'll be surprised to find out a great secret: It's easier that way.

But passing the real test of living a life of Sacred Work will always require extraordinary courage—the courage to transcend the self to serve the other. The only way to fail the challenge, the test of life itself, is not to take it—to retreat to the grandstands and watch passion playing out on the great field below. It will always be tempting to run away, to rest where we are, to give in to inertia and stop trying.

The richest gold of life is the gift of love. Spend it. It will replenish itself. Leave it unspent and you will waste the greatest gift your life has to offer.

The only way to live love is to live our passion, to take the field with all its suffering and joy and to fulfill the demands of others who need our love. We want to know, at the end, that we have made our best effort to improve the lives of others. That we, ourselves, have lived and that we have loved as deeply as we knew how. This is the magic gift, the essential secret of Sacred Work.

SPECIAL SECTION:
THE STATE OF THE ART— BEST PRACTICES ORGANIZATIONS THAT LIVE LOVING CARE

You must be the change you wish to see in the world.

—Gandhi

Fortunately, there are some very special hospitals and charities that are models of *being* the change they want to see in the world. Below is a partial list of state-of-the-art organizations and an honor roll of others that demonstrate the balance of excellence—places where work is seen as truly sacred.

The first list is locally focused. It aims to honor Middle Tennessee Charities served by the Baptist Healing Trust.

The second list is nationally focused and is meant to recognize hospitals and health systems where love is in bloom.

THE STATE OF THE ART—MODELS OF SACRED WORK AMONG MIDDLE TENNESSEE CHARITIES

1) Alive Hospice

With the enlightened leadership of CEO Jan Jones and COO Edie Rimas, Alive Hospice is emerging as one of the top Hospice organizations in the United States. Central to this has been the exceptional work of Vice Presidents Karen York and Debbie Baumgart. Different from many high-level executives who spend lots of time talking about implementation and not really doing anything, this pair has galvanized the loving-care initiative at Alive Hospice by teaching a continuous pattern of courses on loving care, revamping personnel polices consistent with the tools and steps outlined in this book, and infusing in the organization the sense of deep commitment to hospice care as Sacred Work.

Their success distinguishes this organization as a true leader in the practice of Radical Loving Care.

2) Magdalene House

This exceptional charity has been referenced frequently in this work as a model of Radical Loving Care. They have gone against the status quo and risen to a whole new level as one of the premier charities of any kind anywhere in the country. They have published a guide on how to duplicate their work in your city.

Most programs that care for recovering prostitutes/drug addicts report success rates around 30%. Magdalene offers a two-year program with five stages through which women travel. They have achieved a staggering 70% success rate among the 75 women who have entered the program since 1997 and stayed more than a month.

The keys to Magdalene's success are many, but the two core ones are identical to the keys to successful Sacred Work and the establishment of a loving-care community. They are discipline and compassion *in balance.* Women who enter the program receive a *balanced* dose of both. The results speak for themselves.

3) The Siloam Clinic

When I first visited this remarkable home of healing, I was stunned by the humble quality of their offices, which were crammed into a thousand square feet in a rundown apartment building. I couldn't imagine how they could handle eight thousand patients visits (mostly immigrants) a year. "We tell our staff to see the face of Christ in each patient," Nancy West says. After fourteen years of hard work and the generous support of foundations including HCA and the Baptist Healing Trust, Siloam now occupies new quarters in a lovely facility. This has enabled them to expand their mission of service to care for many more people and reduce their waiting list.

If you want to see loving care in action, visit Siloam.

4) Interfaith Dental Clinic

Rhonda Switzer understands the power of a smile. Under her leadership, Interfaith Dental Clinic does more than fix teeth and fill cavities. The loving staff of her clinic delivers regular doses of love and respect to the underprivileged who come for dental care. Many who have been afraid to smile for fear of exposing their crooked teeth now shine with smiles from without and from within.

5) The Campus for Human Development

Father Charles Strobel is one of America's finest angels. For most of his life he has served the poorest of the poor in Middle Tennessee. Following in the footsteps of his late mother, who served the homeless most of her life, Father Strobel has founded a unique and special charity. Going beyond offering a place for overnight lodging for the poor, this Samaritan has overseen the development of programs that teach computer skills to the homeless, care for those who have been discharged from hospitals, and, through an spectacularly successful program called Room at the Inn, has expanded the reach of loving care through hundreds of churches that offer places to stay for those displaced from home and shelter.

HONOR ROLL OF MID-TENNESSEE CHARITIES

1) Oasis

Hal Cato is one of the finest leaders I have encountered in charity work. Intelligent, sophisticated, charming, and committed, he has all the skills and all the heart to lift Oasis to the top rank of American charitable caregiving. The charity he leads focuses on caring for young people adrift in the world because they have been cast out of their homes, have run away voluntarily, or are caught in a web of violence.

Hal is doing a brilliant job of guiding his staff toward excellence.

Within a year's time, I fully expect Oasis to be recognized as a place where Sacred Work is practiced consistently by all staff.

2) McKendree Village

The Healing Trust team has just begun its partnership with this Methodist organization, a giant nursing home and caregiving facility in Nashville. But McKendree is already on the honor roll because of the effective leadership of Jim Robinson, who has already raised consciousness of what he calls Quality Loving Care to the point where caregiving patterns are changing for the better.

3) Outlook Nashville

CEO Mary Givens oversees a staff that looks after adults who are dealing with profound mental and/or physical impairment. Another part of her team looks after medically fragile children. One visit to this organization and you would see why they are already on the honor roll and may soon become a star.

4) Park Center

Our team has only made one visit to this remarkable organization that supports patients with mental illness. Together with other research we have done, we have placed them on our honor roll based on their remarkable history of success in establish a loving-care environment for their staff and patients.

AMERICA'S PREMIER HEALING HOSPITALS

1) Parrish Medical Center, Titusville, Florida (America's #1 Healing Hospital in 2005)

This is the hospital we believe has done the most in developing and applying the elements of Radical Loving Care. The catalyzing force has been the enlightened and progressive leadership of CEO George Mikitarian. George has seen to it that loving care permeates every corner of his organization. His charm, persistence, insight, and willingness to stand strong against skeptics who attempted to undercut this work are a shining example of the power of cultures of Radical Loving Care. In addition, the board of Parrish Medical Center deserves special recognition. They have unanimously and continuously backed the loving-care initiative in the midst of crossfire from a minority who thought it was a waste of time. With the outside help of Dr. Brian Wong's team from Seattle and the Baptist Healing Trust from Nashville, the leadership team continues to reach new heights each day in the enrichment of organizational culture.

In addition, Parrish Medical Center has been nationally recognized for its success in creating a physical environment that is, architecturally, as beautiful and soothing as any of the dozens of hospitals we have visited. Operating within view of the launch pads at Cape Canaveral, this organization has launched itself into the top ranks of America's best Healing Hospitals.

2) St. Charles Hospital, Bend, Oregon

St. Charles is a long-term and widely acclaimed veteran in the practice of loving and patient-centered care. Before many healthcare providers were talking about patient-centered care, St. Charles was living it. Today this two hundred–plus–bed hospital is an international model that demonstrates enormous success in the delivery of patient-centered care. This mecca of Loving Care regularly receives visits from groups all over the country who want to see a culture of sacred work firsthand. The culture of Loving Care has been planted deeply enough to thrive through changes in administration.

3) The Mayo Clinic, Rochester, Minnesota

For many decades now, the Mayo Clinic has offered a model of excellence unparalleled in the western world. Although some of its systems could benefit significantly from deeper attention to loving care, and some of its satellites do not always reflect the full level of Mayo excellence, it remains one of the finest systems of medical care ever developed. Mayo is a place where clinical excellence is balanced with a system whose goal is to treat patients with respect.

4) Johnson City Medical Center, Johnson City, Tennessee

Under the guidance of Dennis Vonderfecht, President and CEO of its holding company, Mountain States Health Systems, 400-bed Johnson City Medical Center has developed into a model of loving strength similar to Parrish Medical Center. With continued improvement, Johnson City has a chance of becoming one of America's premier Healing Hospitals. Mountain States has a terrific mission statement that says they are committed to "Bringing loving care to health care." Their patient-centered focus has brought them recognition as the only Nurse Magnet Hospital in Tennessee, and they continue to strengthen their standards to compete effectively for the Baldridge Quality Award.

5) M.D. Anderson Cancer Hospital, Houston, Texas

Illness often makes us feel weakened and exposed, and cancer creates an exquisite vulnerability. There are many fine cancer treatment centers in America. M.D. Anderson has developed a particularly fine balance of compassion and high-level medical care. Their strong international reputation is well-deserved.

HONOR ROLL OF AMERICAN HOSPITALS

The following hospitals, though perhaps not yet in the top rank of America's Healing Hospitals, have nevertheless made important strides in establishing cultures of loving care. Their work continues.

1) Lourdes Hospital, Paducah, Kentucky

Still early in its effort to grow a rich garden of loving care, Lourdes Hospital has had to deal with significant financial challenges. As it works its way back to fiscal health, this hospital, part of Cincinnati-based Catholic Health Partners, has an excellent chance of becoming a full-fledged Healing Hospital. With the spiritual guidance of Catholic Sisters, lead by Sister Marie Moore, Lourdes has initiated Presence training, established its Committee for Cultural Change, and set up its Target Teams to bring about positive changes in hiring, orientation, and loving care training.

2) Beth Israel-Deaconess, Boston, Massachusetts

In the quarter-century of glory days under the guidance of former CEO Dr. Mitch Rabkin, Beth Israel Hospital was an international model for how to create loving care. Nursing leadership was so effective at Beth Israel that it was viewed by most Boston doctors and nurses as *their* number-one choice for care. Battered by the competition of a merger between Massachusetts General Hospital and Brigham and Womens in the mid-'90s, Beth Israel sustained a body blow to its financial stability. It is now on the recovery path, as CEO Bruce Levy is working to restore the BI to the leadership position it once held. Quality remains strong. If it can re-attain the cultural strength of the Rabkin years, it will take a top leadership position as a Healing Hospital.

3) Riverside Methodist Hospital, Columbus, Ohio

It's always hard to be objective about a place you've once led and lead no longer. I know that from 1983–1995, Riverside Methodist Hospital developed an extraordinary culture of loving care. The best leadership team I've ever seen led that hospital over this period, and it's a crime that the group couldn't stay together even longer.

After a period of relative decline from 1996-2000, Riverside, under the leadership of Bruce Hagan as CEO, Mary Ann Wilcox as Chief Nursing Officer, Dr. Pam Jelly-Boyers, and the guidance of OhioHealth CEO David Blom, Riverside again shows signs of recovering the kind of national leadership it held in the early 1990s as one of America's premier loving-care workplaces. Let's hope this progress continues.

4) Saint Joseph of Orange Health System

Under the leadership of CEO Deborah Proctor and with the enlightened guidance of Nancy Lee and Robin Orr, this fourteen-hospital system is gradually emerging as a leader in the practice of loving care in a faith-based system. Because of the size of the system, the process of culture change is complex. As with others in the early stages of the loving-care movement, time will tell if the Saint Joseph system can truly break into the top ranks of loving-care leadership.

5) Sparrow Health System

Sparrow is headed by a marvelous CEO named, ironically, Swan. Dennis Swan is determined to grow a Healing Hospital in the large organization that dominates healthcare in the Lansing, Michigan, area. His commitment to creating a place of Sacred Work is still in its early stages and the future will reveal whether he can move his large system into the top ranks of America's healthcare organizations.

6) Wuesthoff Health System, Cocoa Beach, Florida

Ever since CEO Emil Miller appointed her to head the system's Loving Care initiative, the biggest difference-maker in this organization has been Senior V.P. Johnette Gindling. With her encouragement, an excellent Steering Committee has been put in place and there has been an organization-wide launch of the Radical Loving Care concept. Although not as far along as their nearby neighbor Parrish Medical Center, Wuesthoff has made some very positive strides in developing a Healing Hospital culture.

7) Baptist Hospital, Nashville, Tennessee

America's very first Healing Hospital from 1998 through 2002, many observers believe this organization slipped a bit between 2003 and 2005. This was a time of merger, leadership transition, and uncertainty. Nevertheless, the organization continued to sustain generally good employee morale and positive patient satisfaction. Under the overall direction of Jim Houser, new CEO of owner St. Thomas Health, there are encouraging signs that Baptist Hospital may one day regain its leadership position among America's Best Healing Hospitals.

8) Sisters of Mary of the Presentation Health System, Sioux City, South Dakota

With the leadership of Sister Suzanne Stahl, V.P. of Mission, and the guidance of my long-time colleague Tracy Wimberly, R.N., this system has quietly woven a beautiful tapestry of loving care among their partner/employees in a system that serves a remote part of the United States. With persistence and loving commitment, their staff has embraced their work as sacred and they now belong on the Honor Roll of America's Healing Hospital Systems.

9) Monroe Carrell, Jr. Children's Hospital at Vanderbilt University, Nashville

CEO Jim Schmerling, working with Terrell Smith and Dr. Rebecca Swan, helped create a breakthrough training program for pediatric residents from the model of Radical Loving Care. In addition, this fine hospital has worked actively and successfully to train staff in the art of loving care.

IN GENERAL NEED OF MAJOR IMPROVEMENT

1. Most university hospitals where the demands of research and teaching have shoved loving care to the sidelines are in need of major improvement.
2. Most large government hospitals such as Cook County Medical Center in Chicago are in need of major improvement. In these giant organizations, loving care is made difficult by the crush of bureaucracy, high patient volumes, and the failure of leadership to understand the importance and possibility of change.

These two groups of organizations are deeply in need of leadership that is willing to recognize that love-based care needs to sit at the center of any great charity.

IN THE END

What is not love is fear.

—Marianne Williamson

As we consider and pursue our own desire to love others as we would like to be loved, inevitable obstacles arise. One of the most remarkable is anger and resentment. One of the forces that promotes these feelings is our natural desire for reciprocity. When we do something kind for another adult, we expect them to do the same in return. When they don't, the dragon of resentment awakens within and creates hostility. Giving up the expectation of reciprocity is one way to ease the strength of the resentment dragon. Yet anger is still bound to come through us. As Williamson suggests, since anger is not love, then it is born of fear. To deal with our fears, we may seek to control the behavior of others. This is terribly difficult. When we fail, we become angry. Anger is also born when we want to say we're scared but don't feel we have permission to do so. We hope people will understand we're scared. Instead, they are offended by our anger and we drive them further away just when we needed them to be closer to us.

Becoming aware of this phenomenon is always the first step toward a solution. As you see anger in others and in yourself, know that it is born from fear, not from love. Respond with love and you will help dissolve this anger in both others and yourself.

ABOUT THE AUTHOR

Erie Chapman, M.T.S., J.D., is president and chief executive officer of the Baptist Healing Trust, Nashville, Tennessee. His first book, *Radical Loving Care,* is now in its sixth printing and is changing the way health care is delivered in America. Across his extraordinary career, he has served as a successful trial attorney, federal prosecuting attorney, night court judge, producer/host of an internationally syndicated television show, publisher of a healthcare magazine, newspaper columnist, radio talk show host, documentary film producer, and author. He is also a prize-winning photographer and a music composer. He is a graduate of Vanderbilt University Divinity School.

The primary focus of Mr. Chapman's career, however, has been in the leadership of hospitals and healthcare organizations. Over twenty-five years of his career, he served as President and CEO of Riverside Hospital in Toledo, Ohio (at age 33), Riverside Methodist Hospital in Columbus, Ohio, the nine-hospital U.S. Health Corporation (now OhioHealth) in Columbus (founding president and CEO), chief operating officer of the publicly traded InPhyNet Medical Management Co., Ft. Lauderdale, and Baptist Hospital System, Nashville. Erie and his wife, Kirsten, a prize-winning journalist and author of *The Way Home,* live in Nashville. They have two children and one grandchild.

Baptist Healing Trust
1919 Charlotte Ave.
Nashville, TN 37203
www.healinghospital.org